Learn Windows® XP, Brief

Richard Alan McMahon, Sr.

Upper Saddle River, New Jersey 07458

Acquisitions Editor: Melissa Whitaker-Oliver
VP Publisher: Natalie Anderson
Assistant Editor: Melissa Edwards
Developmental Editor: Joyce Nielson
Media Project Manager: Cathleen Profitko
Marketing Manager: Emily Williams Knight
Marketing Assistant: Scott Patterson
Manager, Production: Gail Steier de Acevedo
Project Manager: Lynne Breitfeller
Associate Director, Manufacturing: Vincent Scelta
Manufacturing Buyer: Natacha St. Hill Moore
Design Manager: Pat Smythe
Interior & Cover Design: Judy Allen
Full-Service Project Management & Composition: Pre-Press Company, Inc.
Printer/Binder: RR Donnelley & Sons Company
Cover Printer: Phoenix Color Corp.

Microsoft and the Microsoft Office User Specialist logo are trademarks or registered trademarks of Microsoft Corporation in the United States and/or other countries.

Microsoft Excel, Solver, and Windows are registered trademarks of Microsoft Corporation in the U.S.A. and other countries. Screen shots and icons reprinted with permission from the Microsoft Corporation. This book is not sponsored or endorsed by or affiliated with Microsoft Corporation.

Copyright © 2003 by Pearson Education, Inc., Upper Saddle River, New Jersey 07458. All rights reserved. Printed in the United States of America. This publication is protected by Copyright and permission should be obtained from the publisher prior to any prohibited reproduction, storage in a retrieval system, or transmission in any form or by any means, electronic, mechanical, photocopying, recording, or likewise. For information regarding permission(s), write to: Rights and Permissions Department.

10 9 8 7 6 5 4 3 2 1
ISBN 0-13009410-2

This textbook is dedicated to my family—

my wife Sheronna, my daughter Lauren, and my son Ricky—

because without their tolerance and assistance,

it would never have happened.

Learn Windows® XP, Brief

SERIES EDITORS **John Preston, Sally Preston, Robert L. Ferrett**

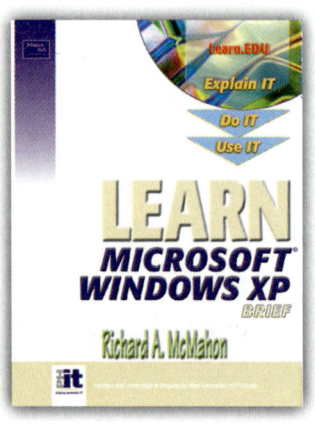 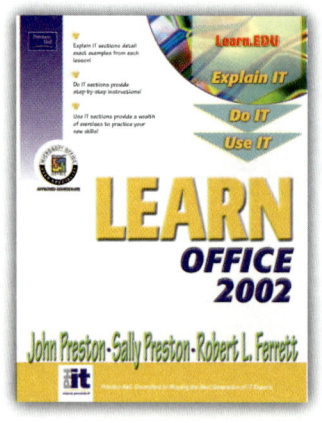 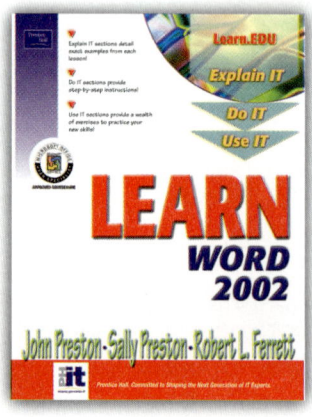

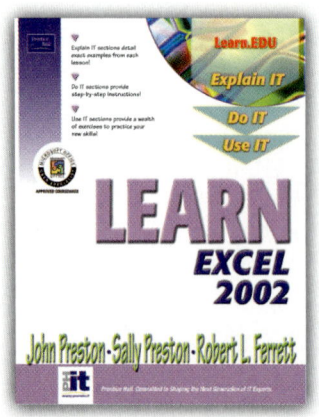 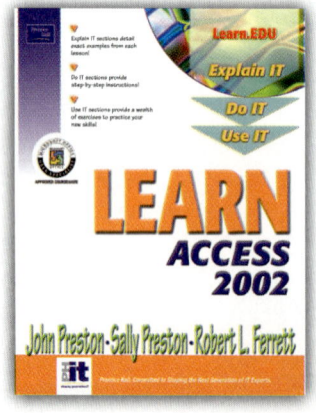 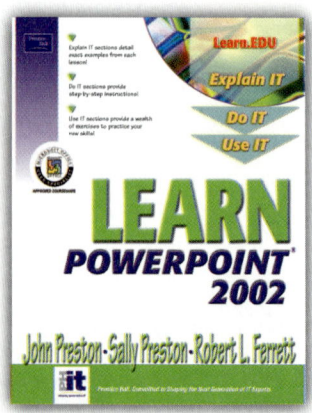

About the Author

Rich McMahon is a full-time lecturer in the Finance, Accounting, and Computer Information Systems Department at the University of Houston–Downtown Campus in Houston, Texas. There he teaches introductory and advanced data communications and networking, systems analysis, information security management, management information systems, business cornerstone, and introductory and advanced computer applications courses. Rich is also an independent consultant for companies in the Houston area and a partner in the M&N Technology Training Center, Inc. that recently opened in Houston, Texas. Rich's current certifications are: Microsoft: MCT, MCSE, MCP, and MCP+I; Novell: CNI, CNE, and CNA; and COMPTIA: CTT+.

Contents

Lesson 1: Getting Started with Windows XP — 1

Explain It — 1
Introduction — 1
Visual Summary — 2

Do It — 3
Task 1   Waking and Logging on to Windows XP — 3
Task 2   Practicing with the Mouse on the Desktop — 6
Task 3   Changing Your Mouse Settings — 9
Task 4   Changing Your Recycle Bin Settings — 12
Task 5   Changing Your Folder Options — 14
Task 6   Changing Your User's Options — 19
Task 7   Logging off Windows XP — 21

Use It — 28
Comprehension — 28
Reinforcement — 30
Challenge — 32
On Your Own — 36

Lesson 2: Working with Folders and Files — 37

Explain It — 37
Introduction — 37
Visual Summary — 38

Do It — 39
Task 1   Using File and Folder Navigation Tools — 39
Task 2   Navigating to the My Documents Folder — 43
Task 3   Switching to the Windows Explorer View — 46
Task 4   Customizing the Start Menu — 50
Task 5   Gathering Hard Drive Details — 53
Task 6   Using the Search Feature — 55
Task 7   Formatting a Floppy Disk — 56
Task 8   Opening and Closing an Application — 59

Use It — 64
Comprehension — 64
Reinforcement — 66
Challenge — 68
On Your Own — 72

Glossary — G-1
Index — I-1

Preface

PHILOSOPHY OF THE *LEARN* SERIES

The Preston-Ferrett *Learn* series is designed for students who want to master the core competencies of particular software in an efficient and effective manner. We use the rubric EDU to organize the text into sections labeled "Explain It," "Do It," and "Use It." The books use extensive visual cues to provide immediate feedback to the students. Each step is accompanied by a figure displaying the result of doing that step. Highlights and callouts identify key screen elements. Steps are divided into paragraphs that give specific directions and paragraphs that explain the results of those actions. Special fonts and colors are used to identify the objects of actions and what the student should type. Deeper understanding is provided in asides called "In Depth." Places where students are likely to go astray are identified by asides labeled "Caution." The series uses visual elements, such as buttons and icons, to make it easier for beginners to learn the software. However, it recognizes that students who need to use the software at work are interested in speed. Asides called "Quick Tips" give directions on how to use keyboard shortcuts to accomplish tasks that are likely to be common in the workplace. The exercises at the end of each lesson promote increasing levels of abstraction similar to those described in Bloom's taxonomy. The "Comprehension" exercises test students' knowledge of the facts and their ability to recognize relationships and visual elements. The "Reinforcement" exercises provide the opportunity to apply these new skills to a different assignment with less-detailed instructions. "Challenge" exercises require students to learn a new skill that is related to the skills covered in the lesson. "On Your Own" provides students with guidelines for applying the newly acquired skills to a unique project of their own. The guidelines specify general requirements to give the student and the instructor a common ground for evaluation but otherwise allow for creativity and innovation. Books in this series give beginners very detailed step-by-step instruction while providing challenging options for more advanced learners.

STRUCTURE OF A *LEARN* SERIES BOOK

Each of the books in the *Learn* series is structured the same and contains elements that explain what is expected, how to do the tasks, and how to transfer this knowledge into daily use. The elements—"Explain It," "Do It," and "Use It"—are described in detail below.

Explain It

Students are provided with a cognitive map of the lesson where they see a list of the tasks, an introduction, and a visual summary.

Introduction
The EDU design relates to the lessons.

Each lesson has an introduction that describes the contents of the lesson to provide an overview of how the tasks are related to a larger concept that is identified by the title of the lesson.

Visual Summary

A visual summary displays the expected results of performing the tasks. Callouts are used to show the student and the instructor where to look in each file to identify the results of following the instructions correctly.

Do It

Once students are oriented to the objective of the lesson and are aware of the expected outcome, they proceed with the task. Tasks begin with an explanation of the relevance of the tasks and are followed by step-by-step, illustrated instructions on how to "Do It."

Why would I do this?

The authors draw upon their experience in education, business, government, and personal growth to explain how this task is relevant to the student's life. Students are motivated to learn when they can relate the task to practical applications in their lives.

Step-by-step instruction

Instructions are provided in a step-by-step format. Explanations follow each instruction and are set off in a new italicized paragraph.

Figures

Each step has an accompanying figure that is placed next to it. Each figure provides a visual reinforcement of the step that has just been completed. Buttons, menu choices, and other screen elements used in the task are highlighted or identified.

Special Notes

Three recurring note boxes are found in the Preston-Ferrett *Learn* series:

An area where trouble may be encountered, along with instructions on how to avoid or recover from these mistakes.

A detailed look at a topic or procedure, or another way of doing it.

A faster or more efficient way of achieving a desired end.

Use It

The end-of-lesson material, "Use It," consists of four elements: "Comprehension"; "Reinforcement"; "Challenge"; and "On Your Own." Students are guided through increasing levels of abstraction until they can apply the skills of the lesson to a completely new situation in the "On Your Own" exercise.

"**Comprehension**": These exercises are designed to check the student's memory and understanding of the basic concepts in the lesson. Next to each exercise is a notation that references the task number in the lesson where the topic is covered. The student is encouraged to review the task referenced if he or she is uncertain of the correct answer. The "Comprehension" section contains the following three elements:

"True/False": True/false questions test the understanding of the new material in the lesson.

"Matching": Matching questions are included to check the student's familiarity with concepts and procedures introduced in the lesson.

"Visual Identification": A captured screen or screens is used to gauge the student's familiarity with various screen elements introduced in the lesson.

"Reinforcement": These exercises which provide practice in the skills introduced in the tasks, generally follow the sequence of the tasks in the lesson. Since each exercise is usually built on the previous exercise, it is a good idea to do them in the order in which they are presented.

"Challenge": These exercises test students' abilities to apply skills to new situations with less-detailed instructions. Students are challenged to expand their skills set by using commands similar to those they've already learned.

"On Your Own": This exercise is designed to provide students with an opportunity to apply what they have learned to a situation of their choice. Guidelines are provided to give students and the instructor an idea of what is expected.

Glossary

New words or concepts are printed in italics and emphasized with color the first time they are encountered. Definitions of these words or phrases are provided in the text where they occur and are also included in the glossary at the back of the book.

SUPPLEMENTS PACKAGE

There are lots of supplements available for both students and teachers. Let's take a look at these now.

Student Supplements

Companion Web site (www.prenhall.com/learn): Includes student data files as well as test questions that allow students to test their knowledge of the material and get instant assessment.

Instructor Supplements

Instructor's Resource CD-ROM: Includes Instructor's Manual, Test Manager, PowerPoint presentations, and solution files, which are available for downloading.

TRADEMARK ACKNOWLEDGEMENTS

All terms mentioned in this book that are known to be trademarks or service marks have been appropriately capitalized. Prentice Hall cannot attest to the accuracy of this information. Use of a term in this book should not be regarded as affecting the validity of any trademark or service mark.

ACKNOWLEDGEMENTS

I would like to acknowledge the extraordinary efforts of all those individuals involved in this project. It never ceases to amaze me just how hard the editors, copy editors, tech editors, development editors, project managers, marketing managers, compositors, publishers, printers, sales personnel, distributors, and campus book representatives (to name but a few) have to work in order to get a multi-faceted project like this into the hands of the reader. In particular, however, a special acknowledgment should go to the two people who took a chance and supported my desire to continue writing. Without their repeated personal support I would not have worked on a project of this magnitude.

Lisa Lehman, who was the book representative for the UHD campus at the time, took a personal interest in getting fellow Houstonians writing for the company she represented. Lisa heard of my interest in writing additional textbooks and decided to champion my becoming a Prentice Hall author. She was persistent and continued searching upcoming projects until the right one surfaced. Then she presented the idea and even helped with the application process. Anyone who knows Lisa knows how tenacious she can be. This project's being offered to me is an outcome of that tenacity.

Jodi McPherson then decided to take a chance. The outcome of that chance is inside the cover of this textbook and the others of this series. Jodi is the one person who probably best knows all the bumps in the road that had to be overcome along the way to printing these texts. Without her backing this project would not have my name on it.

Hopefully, what you read will be worth the outstanding contributions of everyone involved.

Thank you, each and every one of you.

Learn.EDU Features

Books in the *Learn 2002* series follow the Learn.EDU philosophy: Explain It, Do It, and then Use It.

*E*xplain It
EXPLAIN IT sections begin each Lesson. Students learn up front what will be covered in a Lesson and what they can expect to learn from it.

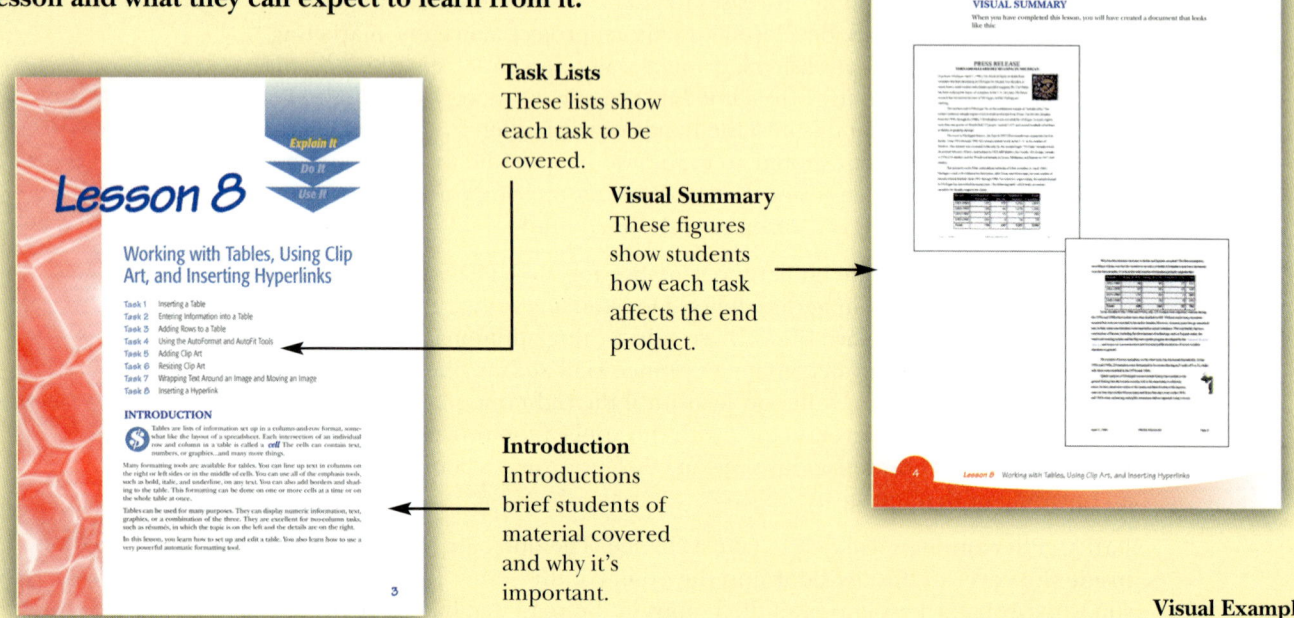

Task Lists
These lists show each task to be covered.

Visual Summary
These figures show students how each task affects the end product.

Introduction
Introductions brief students of material covered and why it's important.

Visual Examples
Numerous screen captures show how the student's own screen should look.

*D*o It
DO IT sections contain numbered steps that walk students through each task, allowing them to do the work themselves along with the instruction.

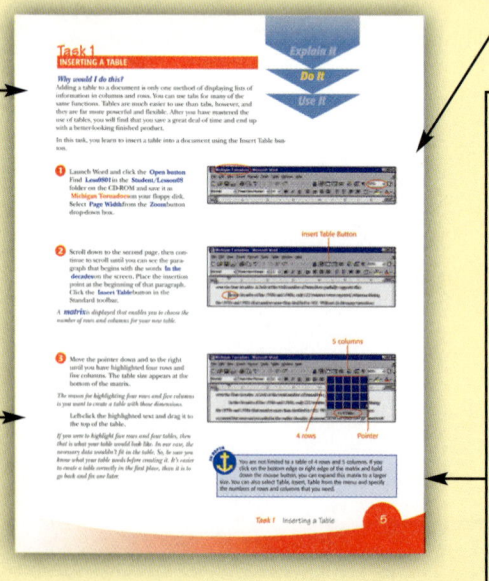

Why would I do this?
These sections explain the relevance to the student of each concept covered.

Numbered Steps
Students are guided through each task in a step-by-step format with explanations in italics.

Quick Tip
A faster or more efficient way of doing something.

In Depth
A detailed look at a topic or procedure, or another way of doing something.

Caution
Troubleshooting tips that point out common pitfalls.

Use It

USE IT sections give the student opportunities to evaluate and practice skills learned in the Lessons, furthering their knowledge, comprehension, and understanding of the topics.

Reinforcement
These exercises provide practice in skills introduced in the tasks.

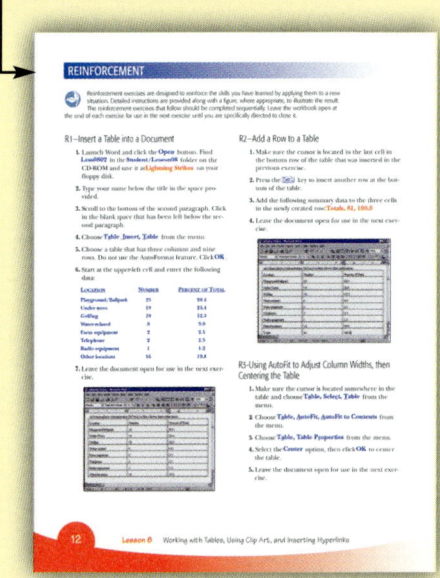

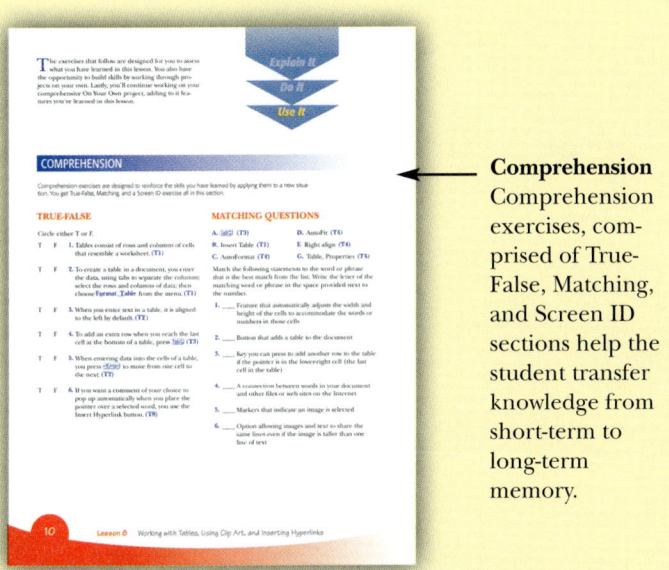

Comprehension
Comprehension exercises, comprised of True-False, Matching, and Screen ID sections help the student transfer knowledge from short-term to long-term memory.

Challenge
The exercises test the student's ability to apply their skills to new situations with less-detailed instructions.

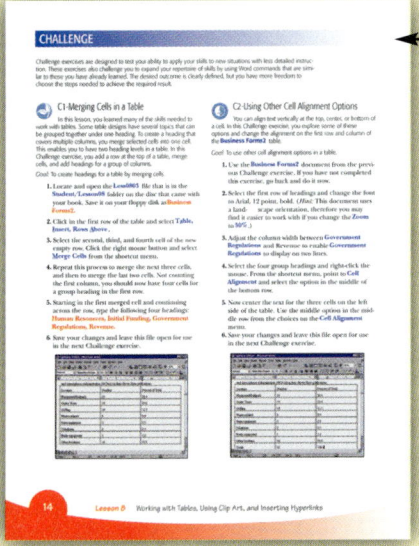

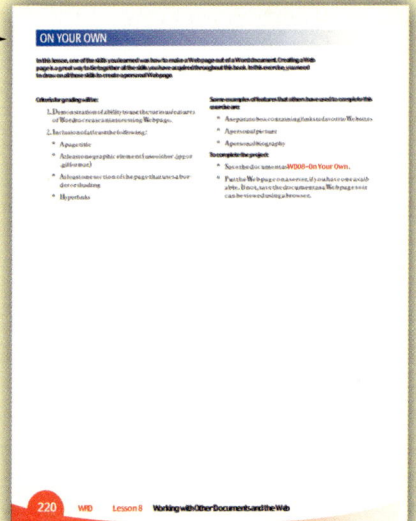

On Your Own
Students are provided with guidelines on how to apply the skills acquired to a project of their choice.

Lesson 1

Getting Started with Windows XP

Task 1   Waking and Logging on to Windows XP
Task 2   Practicing with the Mouse on the Desktop
Task 3   Changing Your Mouse Settings
Task 4   Changing Your Recycle Bin Settings
Task 5   Changing Your Folder Options
Task 6   Changing Your User's Options
Task 7   Logging off Windows XP

INTRODUCTION

Windows XP Professional is different than previous versions of the Windows operating system. Of course, if you are a novice and have never worked with a computer, the whole concept of using any operating system is "different." An *operating system* is software that controls the interface to *peripheral devices* (add-on computer components), allocates storage, schedules tasks, and provides a default interface to the user when no applications are running. Even if you are an experienced Windows user, some components of Windows XP Professional may puzzle you at first. Either way, once you see and use these new components frequently, you will quickly become an avid user of them, as well as the other features Windows XP has to offer.

This lesson gives you the foundations necessary to make the transition from the computer novice (or the more experienced user who is simply curious about what's new), to the seasoned Windows XP Professional user that you'd like to become. We begin this lesson with a computer that is already running with Windows XP as its operating system, and then show you how to gain access to that system. You see how the computer's screen is protected and learn how to wake the system so you can gain computer access through the logon process.

Next, we show you the most important step, logging on. Even experienced users will see some differences when they log on to this newest of Microsoft's operating systems. After the system lets you in, we show you the basic tools you need to know to get started with Windows XP. Those basics include manipulating the graphical interface, practicing with the mouse, and working your way through files and folders.

In this lesson, you learn how to access Windows XP Professional. You also learn how to use the computer's interface and alter some of the operating system's settings and options.

VISUAL SUMMARY

When you complete this lesson, you will have worked with a desktop that looks like this:

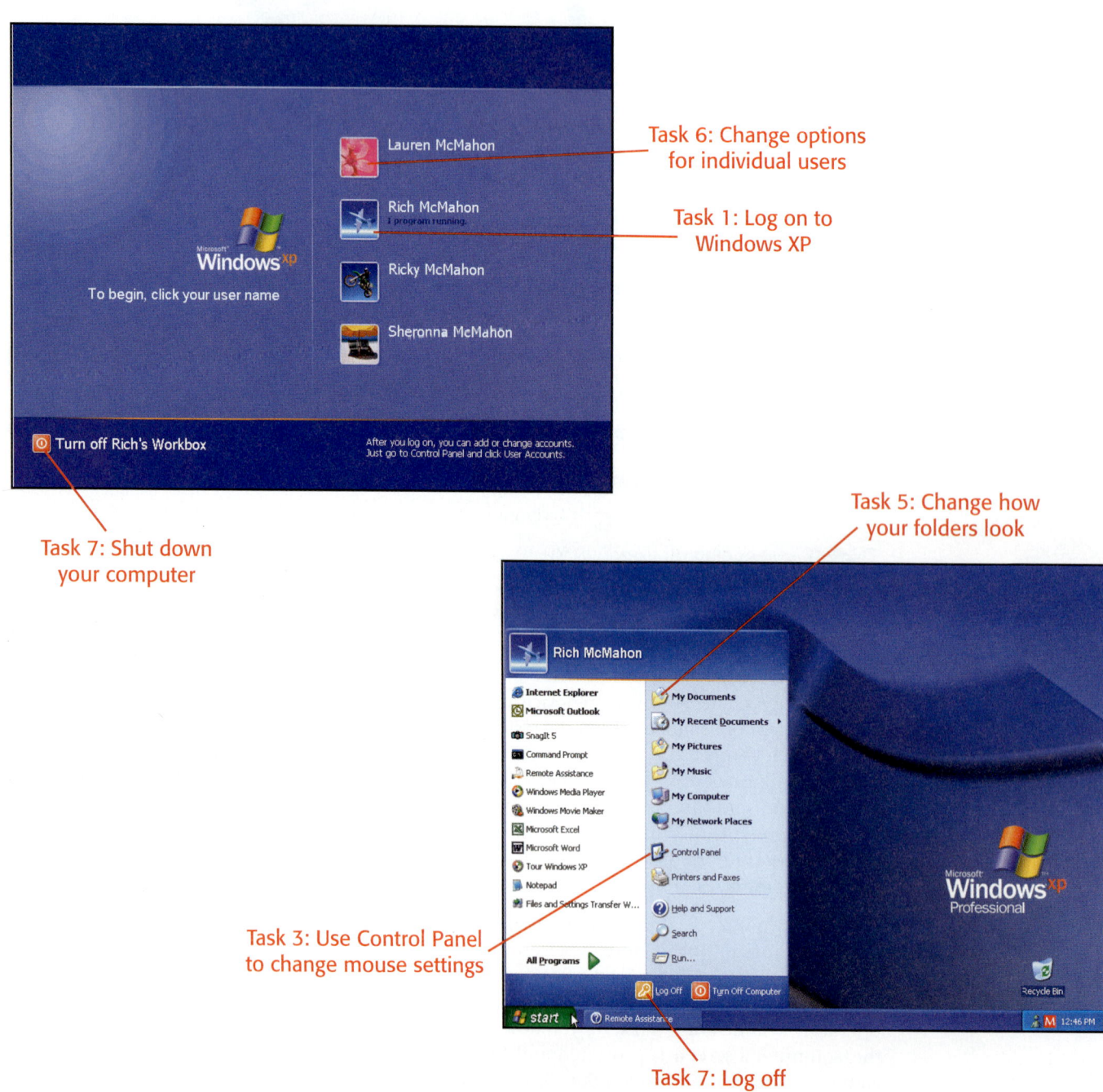

Task 1
WAKING AND LOGGING ON TO WINDOWS XP

Why would I do this?

Windows XP Professional uses a screen saver in its *default* setup (initial settings that are automatically invoked when the operating system is installed). Therefore, if the person in charge of installing and maintaining your computer (usually the *system administrator*) has not changed it, the image you will most likely see first is the system's default screen saver. After you wake the screen saver, you go through the *logon* procedure to gain access to your computer's *desktop*, where you access the applications you use on your computer.

In this task, you learn to wake Windows XP using your mouse, and then you log on to your computer.

❶ Turn on your computer and monitor, if necessary.

Listen to your computer to determine whether it is running. If the computer is on, you should hear a low electrical hum of the cooling fans and computer storage disks coming from the main box where your monitor, keyboard, and mouse are connected. If your monitor is on, it should display a screen saver, the Windows XP desktop, or any other graphic onscreen.

If your monitor is on, but you see a blank screen, determine whether the monitor's power saver is operating.

If a red or amber power-saver indicator light is on, your monitor may be sleeping to conserve power.

Default Windows XP screen saver image

> **IN DEPTH**
> Monitors can have images "burned in" to the reverse side of the glass screen if left on continuously. A screen saver helps avoid forming these images and thus, helps "save" your screen. Screen savers are small computer programs that run in the background without degrading or appreciably slowing down the computer's operating capability.

Task 1   Waking and Logging on to Windows XP   WIN   3

2 Once your computer is on and you have determined that your monitor is working (or simply asleep conserving power), move the mouse across the mouse pad or your desk.

Moving the mouse should awaken your computer from its sleep or power conservation mode, or snap it out of the screen saver mode. You are now ready to log on (request access) to your computer from the **Windows Welcome screen***, which is typically the first screen you encounter when logging on to a Windows XP computer.*

List of all users for this computer
Windows Welcome screen

> Although not a recommended practice (due to its lack of security), your computer could also be set up such that no users other than yourself are planned to work there. In that case, you may not see a list of users, and your access to the computer could be granted immediately. You could, therefore, find yourself right at the desktop directly from the screen saver, with no logon required.

3 *Point* to (move your mouse so the tip of the onscreen arrow touches) your user name on the Windows Welcome screen. (If you don't see a list of user names similar to what is shown in the figure, skip to Task 2. Or, if you see a Log On to Windows dialog box, type your user name and password in the spaces provided, then use your mouse to point to the OK button and click the left mouse button; proceed to Task 2.)

Passing your mouse pointer over your user name (the name your instructor has assigned to you) highlights your name. The **mouse pointer** *is a graphical symbol that allows you to point to objects on the desktop by moving the mouse. Notice too that pausing your mouse pointer over a name may reveal a pop-up information box with a message about any items you had left open (still in use or operating) the last time you worked on the computer. You'll see more of these pop-up information boxes later in this lesson, because they show you some of the context-based assistance built into Windows XP.*

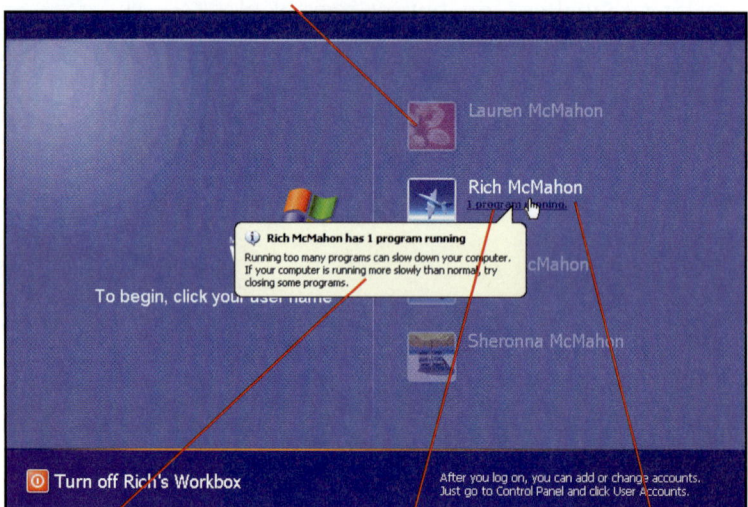

Other users dimmed

Pop-up message   Number of programs left running   Your user name highlighted (brightened)

> **CAUTION** If there are significant numbers of programs or multiple users with programs still running, you may need to close the files and applications, shut the computer down, and then restart it so that your system's operation is not degraded. If this is necessary, ask your instructor for help.

> Other options can occur when logging into Windows XP. A password may be required to verify your identification. If you need one, a password should have been given to you prior to starting this lesson. Additionally, if you are part of a **network** (a group of interconnected computers working together), the screen presented for log on could be the Log On to Windows dialog box, where you have to type your user name and password, and then click OK to get to the desktop.

4 Click your user name on the Windows Welcome screen.

A white password entry box displays, with two buttons on its right side—a green arrow and a blue question mark. If no password is associated with your user name, clicking your user name may display the desktop (the area where you will work, explained later in this lesson).

Type in your user password, if prompted.

In Windows XP, passwords are **case-sensitive**. *Therefore, you must enter the exact combination of uppercase and lowercase letters used when the password was created. A dot appears onscreen in place of each character you type.*

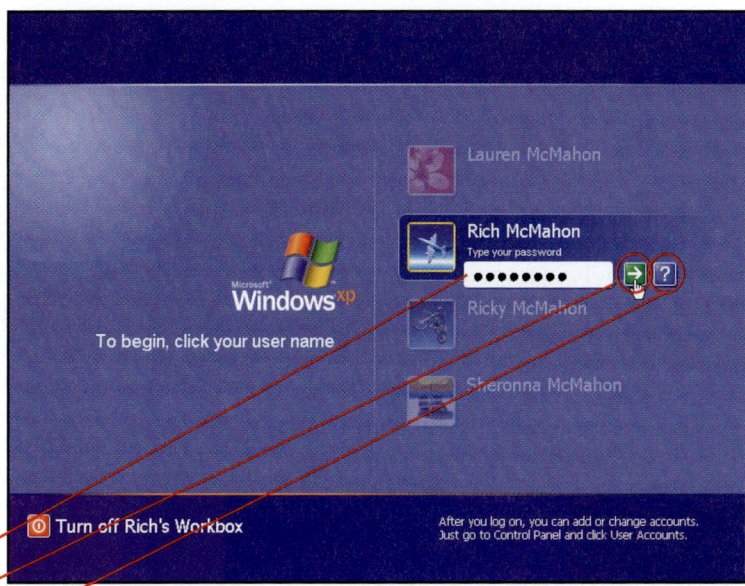

Password entry box with characters dotted out
Green arrow button
Blue question mark button

> **IN DEPTH**
> If you need help remembering your password, assistance may be available on the Windows Welcome screen. If your administrator associated a **hint** with your password, you can click the blue question mark button to view a hint that should remind you of your password. Anyone with access to the computer can view a password hint, even before they log on. Therefore, your hint should remind you of your password without giving it away to anyone else.

5 Click the green arrow button.

Clicking on the arrow button submits your password and, if it is correct, the desktop displays. The desktop you see may not look exactly like the one shown in the figure. Also, different users or desktops may be used in subsequent tasks to emphasize their availability.

> **CAUTION**
> When entering your password, you should be aware of anyone around you close enough to observe what you are typing. The letters are dotted out on your screen but your keystrokes, as you type the letters themselves, can still be observed and imitated later to gain access in your name.

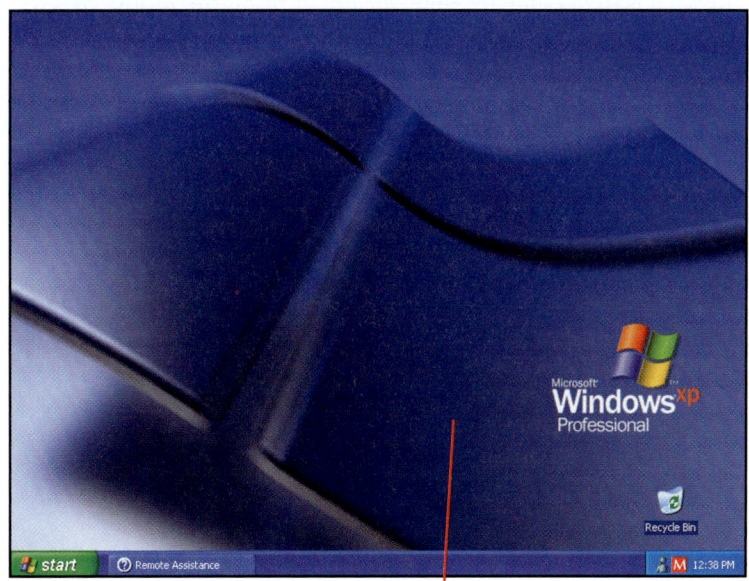

Clean Windows XP desktop

Task 1   Waking and Logging on to Windows XP   WIN

Task 2
PRACTICING WITH THE MOUSE ON THE DESKTOP

Why would I do this?
With the mouse, you invoke computer commands using a graphical, rather than a text-based, interface. That graphical interface is commonly called a *GUI (Graphical User Interface)* and it includes the desktop, as well as other standard Windows features addressed later in this lesson, such as the menu bar, toolbar, address bar, and taskbar.

Use the mouse to first point at the item with which you want to work. Pointing at an object using the mouse pointer allows you to take any of several actions upon that object, including the following:

Click—Press and release the left mouse button. You can use this action to select an object or to place a *cursor* in the intended location.

Drag and drop—Press and hold the appropriate mouse button down (either the left or right button, depending on the intended action) while you drag (move) the object to another location, and release the mouse button. You typically use this action to move objects to another location.

Double-click—Quickly press and release the left mouse button twice in succession. You typically use this technique to execute an action, such as highlighting a word in a document.

Triple-click—Quickly press and release the left mouse button three times in succession. You can utilize this action inside text to highlight a block of text, such as a paragraph.

Right-click—Press and release the right mouse button. You use this action to activate a context-sensitive menu, called a *shortcut menu*, which applies to the intended object.

In this task, you work on increasing your mouse movement accuracy and speed. The goal is to become more proficient at using the mouse to select and move onscreen items.

① Move your mouse and position your mouse pointer in the bottom-left corner of your desktop (your onscreen work area for Windows XP), above the Start button.

Moving the mouse helps you to locate your mouse pointer. If the mouse pointer goes off the screen in any direction, just move your mouse in the opposite direction until the pointer reappears.

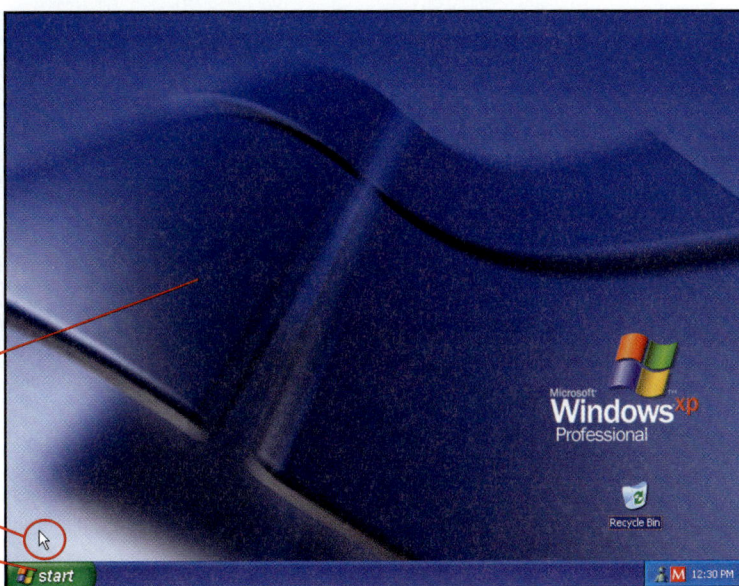

Part of the graphical user interface—the desktop

Mouse pointer
Start button

② Move the mouse in one quick diagonal motion (so the mouse pointer moves toward the opposite corner) and end at the upper-right corner of your monitor.

Your goal is to increase your accuracy when using the mouse to increase the speed with which you accomplish tasks on the desktop.

Keep moving the mouse diagonally from one corner to the opposite corner. Then, try going horizontally or vertically with your mouse to another corner and then diagonally again.

You should quickly feel comfortable with these movements and master this accuracy task. Your speed will increase as a result.

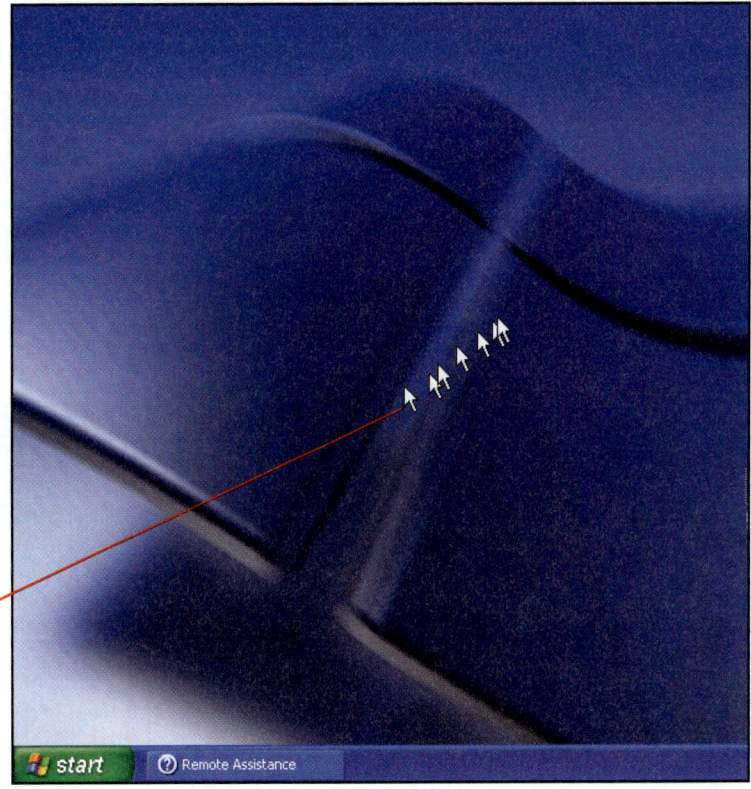

Diagonal mouse movement

⚓ **IN DEPTH**

For emphasis, the figure shows the diagonal movement of the mouse by use of the **Display pointer trails** option that you can select when you personalize your computer's settings through the Control Panel. (You will learn more about the Control Panel in Task 3.) Your mouse configuration will most likely not include being set to show these trails. They are displayed here only to show mouse movement in a diagonal direction.

Task 2 Practicing with the Mouse on the Desktop   WIN   7

3 Click the **Recycle Bin** icon and hold down the mouse button as you drag the icon to the center of your desktop. Then, release the mouse button to drop your icon onto your desktop.

Notice that while moving your icon, its old position is marked by a ghost image until you release the Recycle Bin in its new location.

Pick up and move your **Recycle Bin**, first diagonally and then horizontally (and vertically), using the techniques practiced with just the mouse pointer.

You should quickly feel comfortable with object movements and master this task as you further your mouse proficiency.

Old position ghost icon
Taskbar

IN DEPTH

The Recycle Bin is an *icon* (a small graphic representation of an item) that most likely appears near the lower-right corner of the desktop, just above the taskbar. (The *taskbar* is the bar whose default position is along the bottom of the screen, where the Start button is located.) Single clicking on the Recycle Bin icon should simply select it for your subsequent use. If your defaults have been changed, however, a single click on any item could actually activate it instead of just selecting it. It will become immediately obvious to you which way your settings have been configured upon initial use. You will learn more about the Recycle Bin feature in Task 4.

4 Click the **Start** button one time.

*Clicking the **Start button** opens the **Start menu**, which provides access to numerous menu items and applications.*

Click the **Start** button once again.

This closes the Start menu and the item listing disappears.

QUICK TIP

A quick way to open or close the Start menu is to press ⊞, the *Windows logo key*. Provided your computer's keyboard has one, this key is located between the Ctrl key and the Alt key, and has the Windows logo symbol on the key itself.

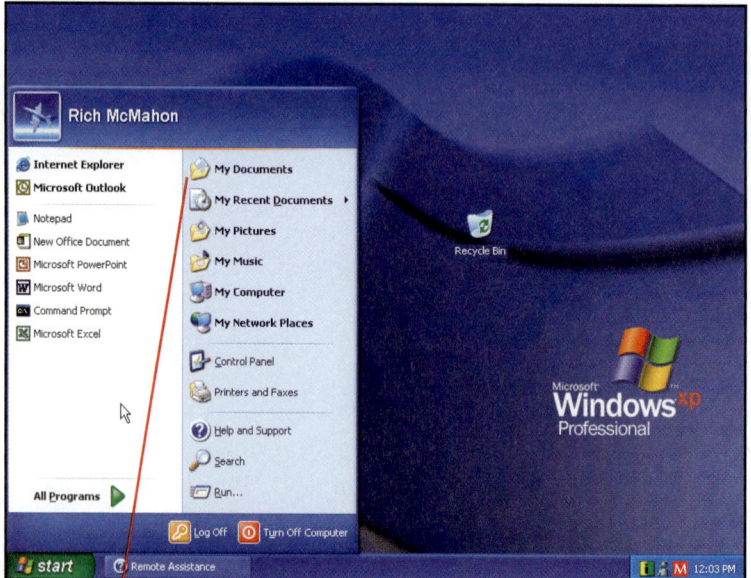

Start menu opened

8 WIN Lesson 1 Getting Started with Windows XP

5 Point to the green **All Programs** arrow.

This opens the All Programs menu showing the applications available on your computer.

All Programs menu opened

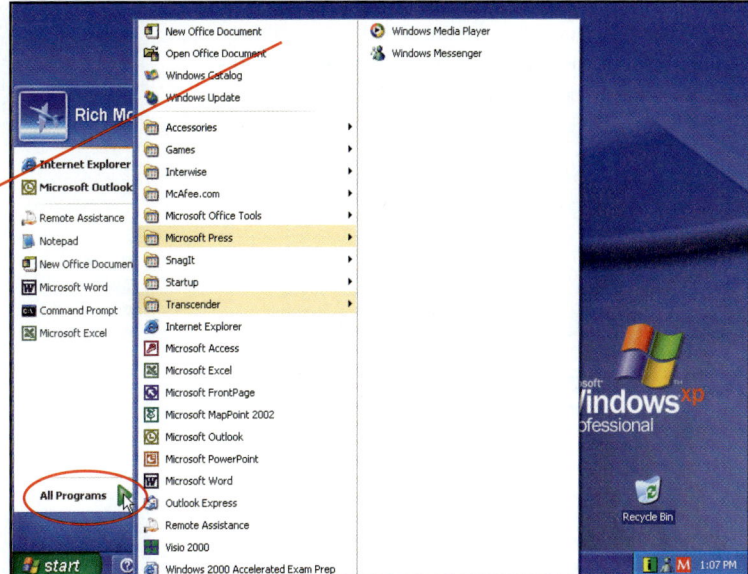

6 Point to the small black arrow to the right of the **Accessories** menu item.

This opens the Accessories menu showing the accessories available on your computer. Notice the accessory items and additional submenus of more accessories available for your use.

Click the **Start** button again.

This closes the Start menu.

Accessories menu opened

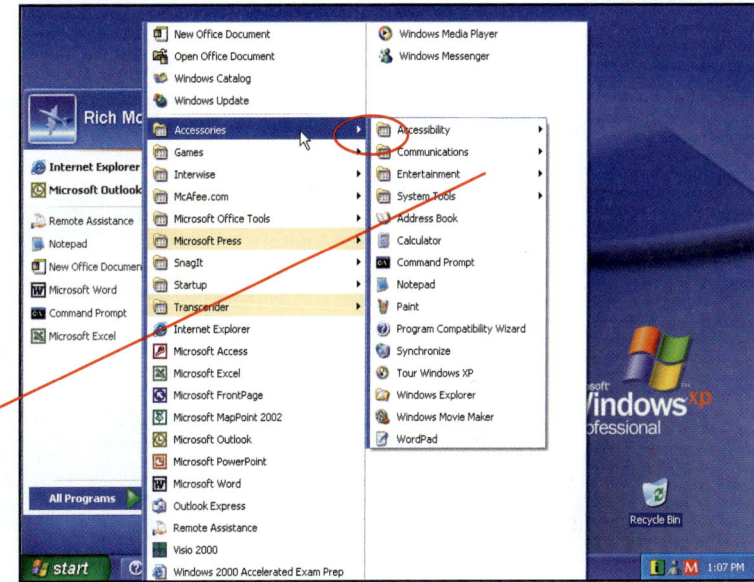

Task 3
CHANGING YOUR MOUSE SETTINGS

Why would I do this?
Having the ability to alter an item's settings is a way of customizing your environment. Windows XP gives you an abundance of items whose settings you can alter to suit your needs or desires. Since you use the mouse frequently, you should know where its settings reside.

In this task, you use keystrokes to work with your mouse settings. Although the quickest way to perform this task (for most individuals) is by using the mouse, using keystrokes as indicated will help you become familiar with an alternative technique for accomplishing tasks.

Task 3   Changing Your Mouse Settings   WIN   9

❶ Press . (If your keyboard doesn't have this key, use the Ctrl+Esc key combination—press and hold down the Ctrl key, and then press the Esc key.)

This opens your Start menu.

> **IN DEPTH**
>
> Notice that the *pop-up descriptions* (small boxes of information that "pop up" when you pause your pointer on some objects) are shown in this task. Although they will not be displayed using the keystrokes specified, they are visible when either using the arrow keys to navigate the first step or when using the mouse. They are shown throughout this task for clarification purposes only.

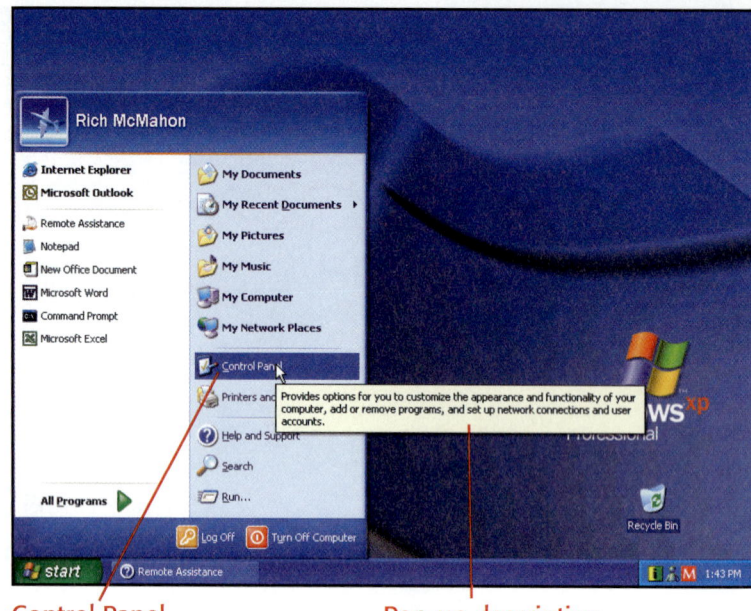

Control Panel — Pop-up description

❷ Press C.

*This opens the Control Panel window. The **Control Panel** is a feature that enables you to change many of your computer's settings using the Windows XP management tools stored there.*

Title bar   Menu bar   Address bar

Toolbar

Printers and Other Hardware icon

Left pane   Right pane   Pop-up description

> **IN DEPTH**
>
> Notice that the name "Control Panel" is shown in the bar along the top of the opened folder (commonly called a ***window***). That bar is called the ***title bar***, and is an integral part of folder navigation (a means of finding and working with items on your computer).
> Also notice that the Control Panel window is divided into various sections, available for you to choose where you want to work. They are arranged in left and right panels or frames (also called ***panes***). In the top section of the window, you see the menu bar, toolbar, and address bar. The ***menu bar*** provides access to menu commands. The ***toolbar*** consists of a row of ***toolbar buttons*** (icons), which allow you to perform tasks more quickly than using the menu bar. The ***address bar*** provides a drop-down list that you can use to access or search for resources either locally or on a network (including the Internet). On the left of your screen, available information items are grouped together. And in the right frame are the objects you will use.

10   WIN   Lesson 1   Getting Started with Windows XP

③ Press the Tab key repeatedly until you highlight **Printers and Other Hardware**, then press Enter.

This opens your Printers and Other Hardware folder and places a Printers and Other Hardware button in the taskbar.

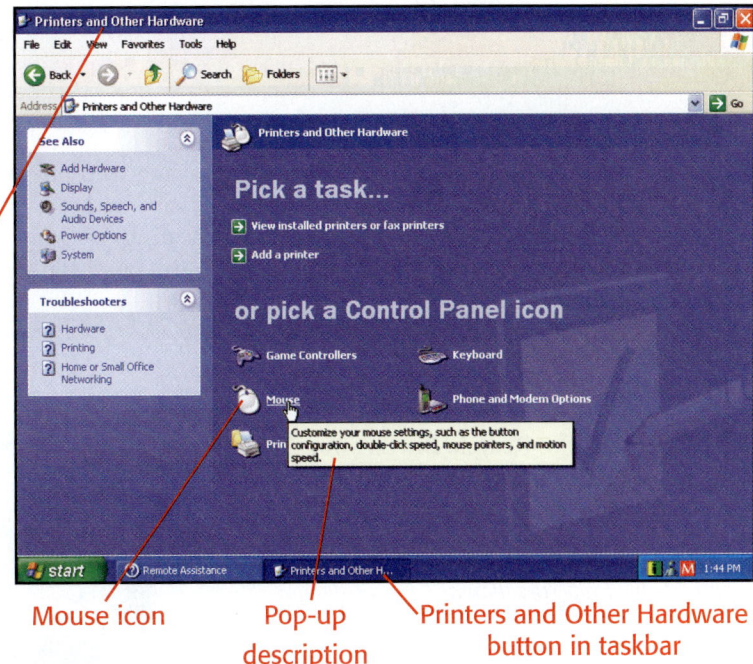

Printers and Other Hardware window

> **IN DEPTH** Notice that highlighting an object using the Tab key puts a faintly visible box around that object, and that pressing Enter is the same as clicking on the object with your mouse.

Mouse icon   Pop-up description   Printers and Other Hardware button in taskbar

④ Press your Tab key repeatedly until you highlight the **Mouse** icon, then press Enter.

This opens the Mouse Properties dialog box. Notice the selection of mouse settings that you can change.

Press your Tab key repeatedly to highlight the **Cancel** button, and press Enter.

This closes the Mouse Properties dialog box and brings you back to the Printers and Other Hardware folder.

Press the Alt key, press F, and then press C.

These keystrokes activate the menu bar, select its File option, and then Close the Printers and Other Hardware folder. These actions bring you back to the desktop.

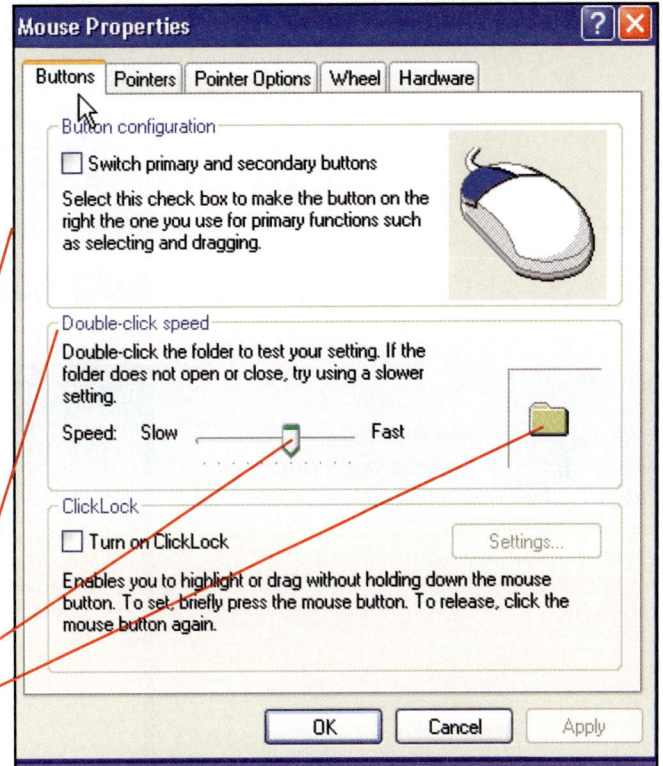

Mouse Properties dialog box
Double-click speed section
Double-click speed adjustment slider
Speed testing folder

> **IN DEPTH** You can slide the Speed adjustment slider in the middle of the Mouse Properties dialog box and test the new speed by double-clicking on the test folder on the right. Notice that the folder opens and closes when you double-click it. Adjust the speed to where it is comfortable for you, then click OK.

Task 3   Changing Your Mouse Settings   WIN   **11**

Task 4
CHANGING YOUR RECYCLE BIN SETTINGS

Why would I do this?

While you are changing settings as a way of customizing your environment, one of the easiest items to change is sitting right there on your desktop—your *Recycle Bin*. Too often, users forget that they can change settings on some of the items that they work with the most, such as their Recycle Bin, and that those settings can be set to suit their own tastes.

In this task, you learn how to change the settings on your Recycle Bin.

1 Right-click the **Recycle Bin** on your desktop, and slide down the shortcut menu to **Properties**.

This displays the Recycle Bin's shortcut menu and highlights the Properties option.

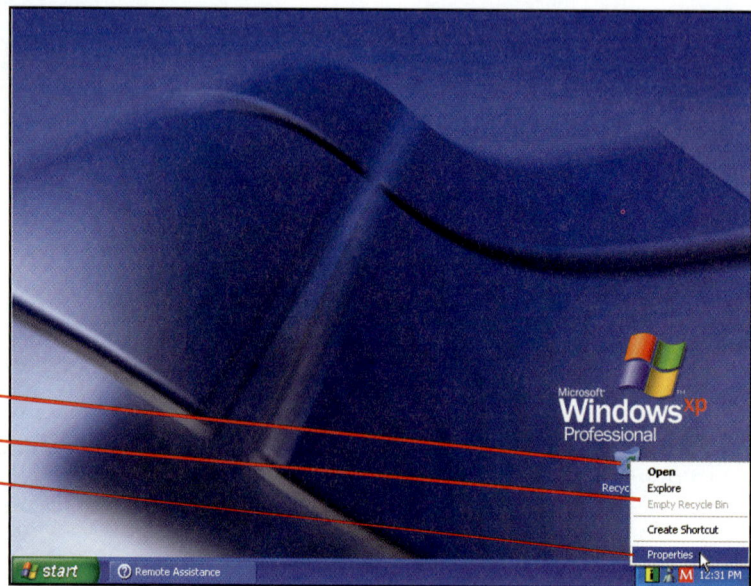

Recycle Bin icon
Shortcut menu opened
Properties option highlighted

2 Click on **Properties**.

This opens the Recycle Bin Properties dialog box and displays what should be the default settings (unless they have been altered either by the administrator or another person using your user identification) with the Global tab open.

Global tab

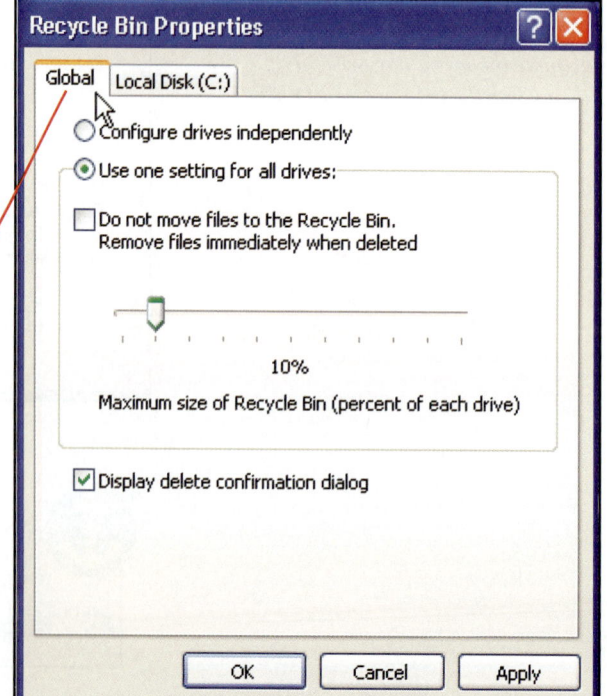

12   WIN   Lesson 1   Getting Started with Windows XP

❸ Select the **Do not move files to the <u>R</u>ecycle Bin** check box, and uncheck the **<u>D</u>isplay delete confirmation dialog** check box.

These actions change two of the default Recycle Bin settings.

Remove check from this option

Select this check box

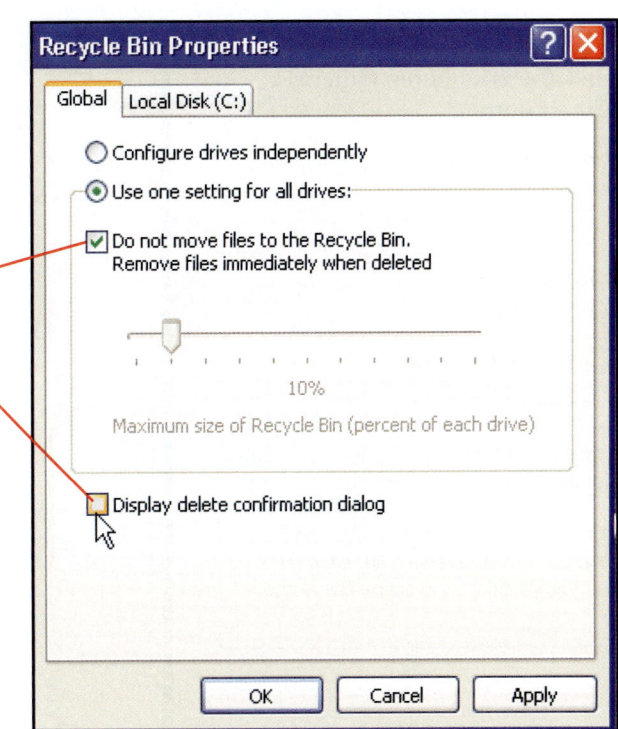

IN DEPTH

If you select the **Do not move files to the Recycle Bin** check box, you will not be given the option of later removing a deleted item from the Recycle Bin. You also should be aware that deselecting the **Display delete confirmation dialog** check box tells the system to immediately discard anything you delete. Normally, when you press Del, Windows XP asks "Are you sure?" and you must confirm the request. Removing the default check mark from this option says that you do not need that reminder.

❹ If you have permission to make changes on your computer, click the **<u>A</u>pply** button. Otherwise, skip to Step 5.

Most dialog boxes have multiple tabs that are used for different setting configurations. If you have permission to make the changes, clicking the <u>A</u>pply button applies your selections but keeps the dialog box open so you can make additional changes or check other settings. Otherwise, clicking the Cancel button cancels any actions you had pending and closes the dialog box.

Apply button

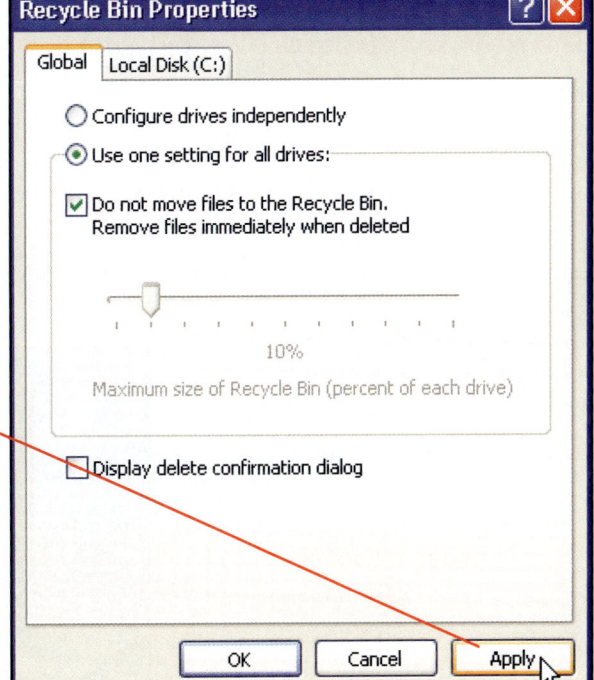

Task 4   Changing Your Recycle Bin Settings   WIN   **13**

⑤ If you have permission to make these changes, click the **OK** button. Otherwise, click the **Cancel** button.

The dialog box closes and you return to the desktop.

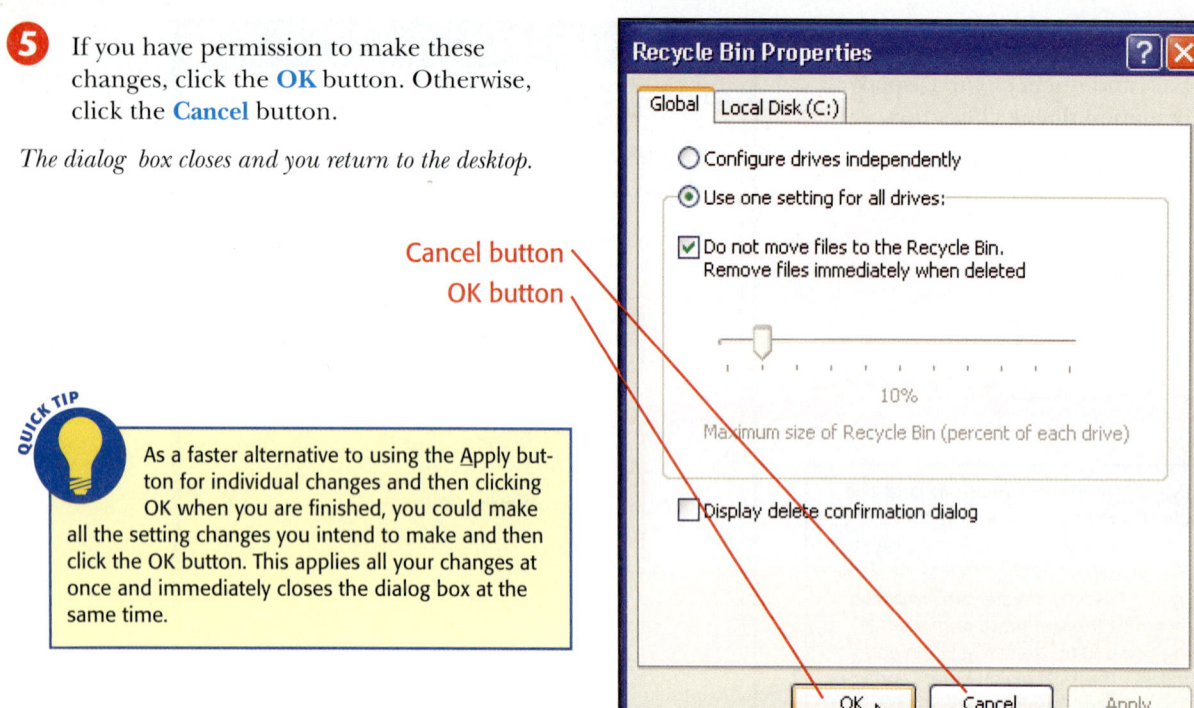

Cancel button
OK button

QUICK TIP
As a faster alternative to using the Apply button for individual changes and then clicking OK when you are finished, you could make all the setting changes you intend to make and then click the OK button. This applies all your changes at once and immediately closes the dialog box at the same time.

Task 5
CHANGING YOUR FOLDER OPTIONS

Why would I do this?

Another setting you can alter to customize your environment deals with the way folders appear when you use them. Even a small change may make it much easier for you to organize or find the objects you frequently use while working on your computer.

In this task, you learn how to change your computer's folder options.

Cascading submenu

❶ Right-click on a blank area in the middle of your desktop and slide to the **New** option.

This opens a shortcut menu and then a cascading submenu from its side.

Folder option highlighted
New option highlighted on shortcut menu

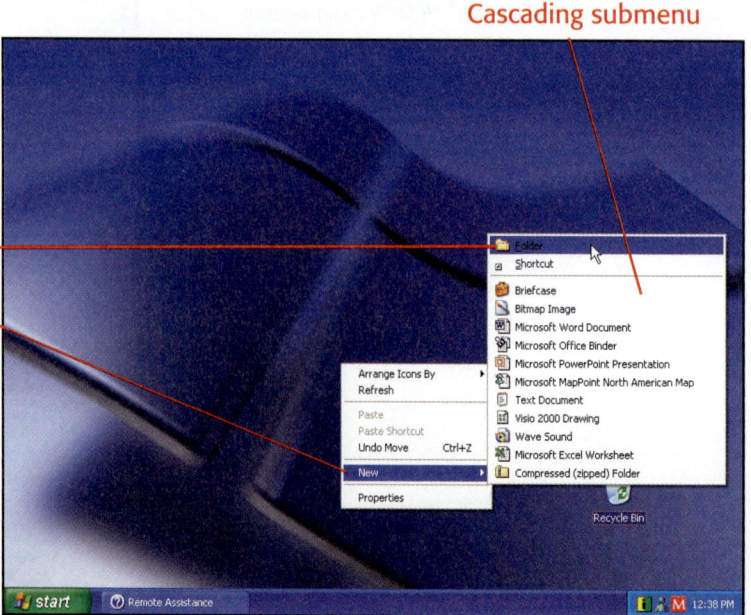

14   WIN   Lesson 1   Getting Started with Windows XP

② Slide to and click the **Folder** option.

This creates a new folder on your desktop. Notice that the object's name is already highlighted.

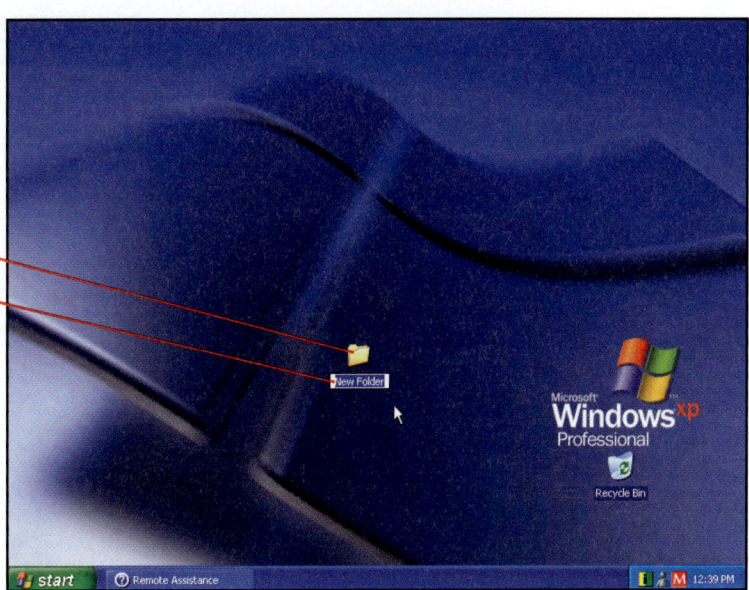

New Folder object
Object's name highlighted

QUICK TIP

Notice that when you create a new object, the name is already highlighted and ready for you to change it (as long as you have not clicked anywhere after creating the object). Begin typing the object's name immediately after creating it. If you click anywhere else, the name is no longer highlighted. If this happens, you can right-click the icon and select Rename from the shortcut menu to highlight the name so you can change it.

③ While the name is still highlighted, type in the object's name: **Folder Settings**.

This puts you in the text editing mode and lets you replace the folder's default name (New Folder) with the name you type (Folder Settings). If you make a mistake while typing, you can use the `←Backspace` *key, or press* `Esc` *to disregard all you entered.*

Press `↵Enter`.

This applies the name you typed to the new folder you created and exits the text editing mode.

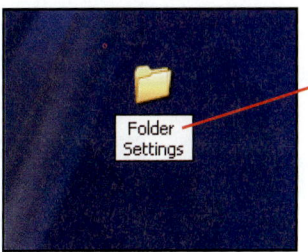

Folder's name replaced

④ Double-click the new **Folder Settings** icon, and then click on **Tools** in the menu bar.

The Folder Settings folder appears in its own window, and the Tools drop-down menu opens. If your new Folder Settings folder was still highlighted, you could also press `↵Enter` *to open the folder.*

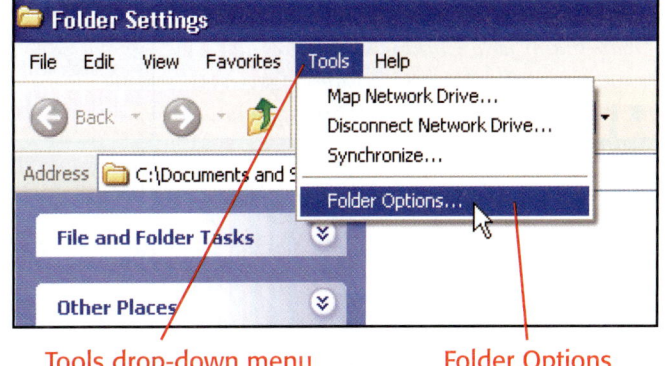

Tools drop-down menu   Folder Options selection highlighted

IN DEPTH

You can use the `Alt` key and the underlined letters provided in the menu items to activate the desired drop-down menu item. For example, pressing `Alt`, then pressing `T` opens the Tools drop-down menu. When you press the `Alt` key, notice that the Tools option in the menu bar changes to Tools. The letters you use to invoke the menu items are sometimes referred to as ***hotkeys***.

Task 5   Changing Your Folder Options   WIN   **15**

5 Slide down the <u>T</u>ools drop-down menu, and click on <u>F</u>older <u>O</u>ptions.

This opens the Folder Options dialog box.

> **CAUTION**
> Remember that your administrator or another user may have changed your default settings prior to your performing this task. Therefore, your settings may not be the same as indicated. If so, you can still perform this exercise but do not alter any settings without permission.

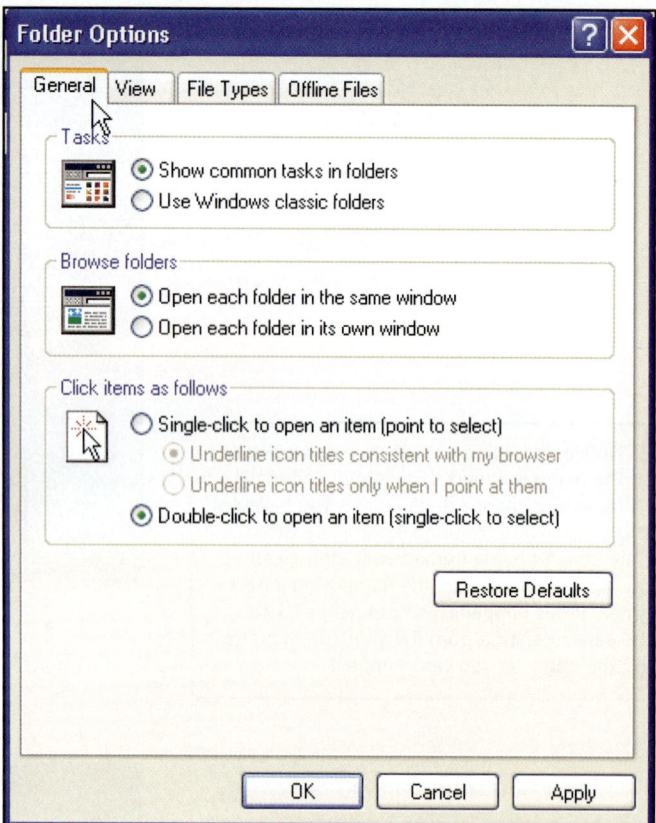

6 Click the **Open each folder in its own <u>w</u>indow** option button and (only if you have permission to apply changes to your computer) click the **OK** button; otherwise, click the **Cancel** button.

Whether you choose to open your folders in their own window or have each consecutive window open in the same space is a preference you have to determine after much computer use. Having separate windows can get confusing, but not having the windows you need open can be unproductive as well. Clicking OK applies all the changes you have selected. Clicking Cancel ignores any changes you made. Either selection returns you to the Folder Settings window.

Folder option button
Apply button
Cancel button
OK button

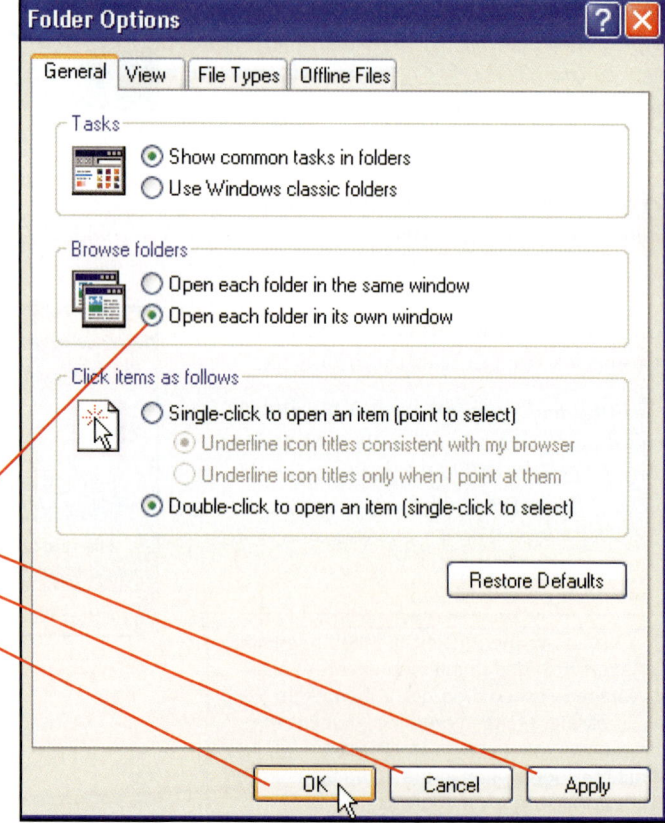

> **CAUTION**
> Do not click the <u>A</u>pply button or the OK button unless you have permission to alter the settings on your computer.

16 WIN Lesson 1 Getting Started with Windows XP

 Click the **Close** button in the Folder Settings window.

*The **Close button** is the small red X button at the far-right side of the title bar. Clicking it closes the Folder Settings window and returns you to the desktop.*

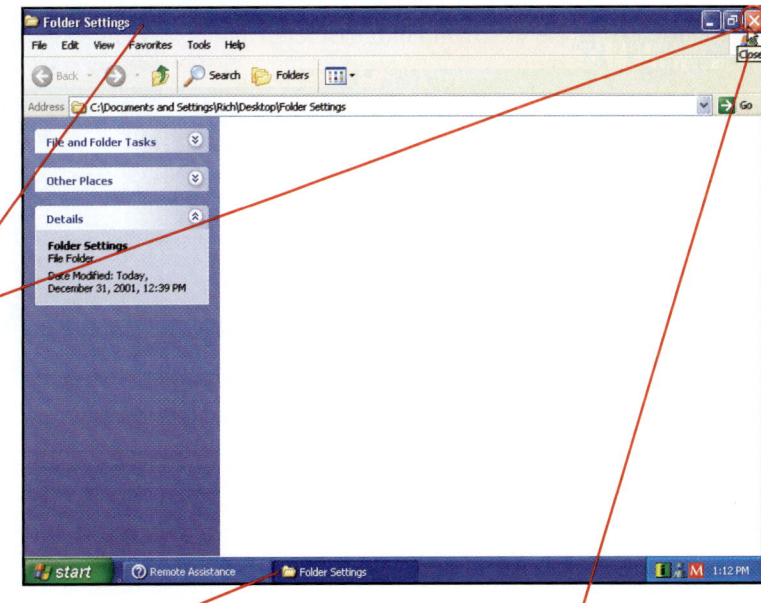

Title bar
Close button

You can also close the window by clicking on the menu bar's File option, and then selecting Close.

Button in taskbar   Pop-up description

 Right-click the **Folder Settings** folder, then click on **Delete**.

This opens the shortcut menu and initiates a delete action to remove the folder from your desktop.

Folder Settings folder
Shortcut menu
Delete option
Empty Recycle Bin icon

Notice whether or not there are items indicated as being stored in your Recycle Bin. If there are, the icon will show items overflowing from the top of the trash can.

Task 5   Changing Your Folder Options   WIN   **17**

9 Click **Yes** in the Confirm Folder Delete dialog box.

If your default Recycle Bin settings have not been altered, this deletes your new Folder Settings folder from your desktop and puts it in your Recycle Bin.

Folder Settings folder
Confirm Folder Delete dialog box
Yes button

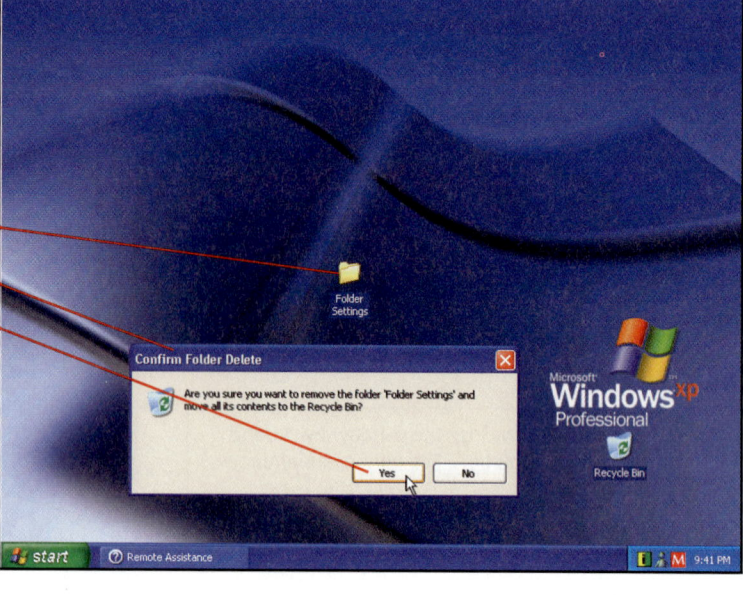

 Remember that, depending on the Recycle Bin settings, you may not get a confirmation when you delete the folder from your desktop.

10 Right-click on your **Recycle Bin** icon, and click the **Empty Recycle Bin** option.

The Confirm File Delete dialog box displays.

Click **Yes**.

This deletes your file (and any others in the Recycle Bin at the time) and returns you to the desktop.

Confirm File Delete dialog box
Yes button
Recycle Bin icon with deleted items

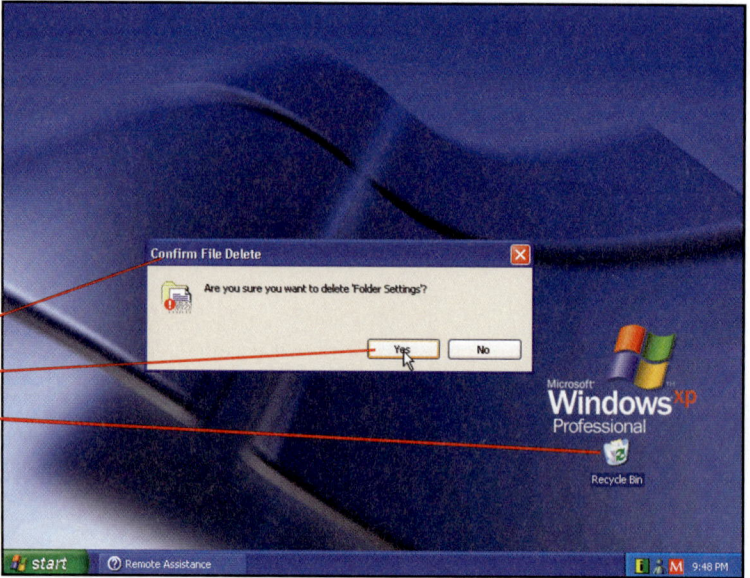

Only empty the Recycle Bin when you are sure you won't need any of the deleted items again. This action removes all items currently stored in the Recycle Bin, and you will no longer be able to restore them without employing additional measures (such as use of additional software or system functions).

Task 6
CHANGING YOUR USER'S OPTIONS

Why would I do this?
You have already seen several settings and numerous options that you can set to customize your working environment. Windows XP lets you go a step further and even alter the way your user name is represented when working on your computer.

In this task, you learn how to change your user's options.

1 Click the **Start** button.

This opens the Start menu.

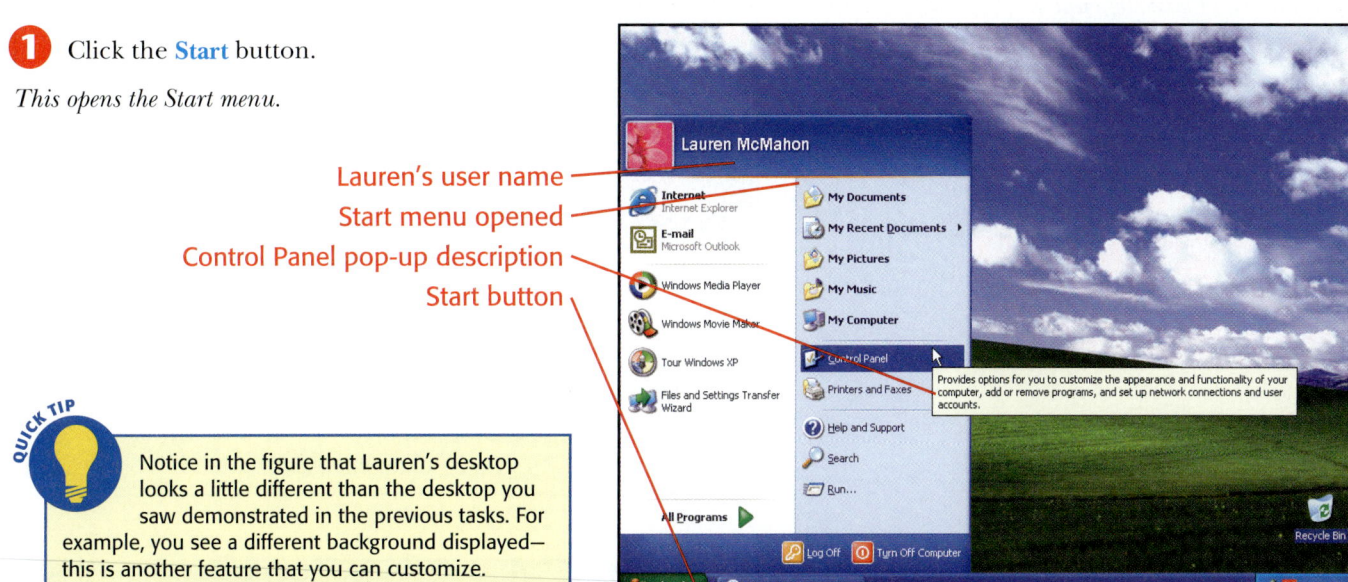

- Lauren's user name
- Start menu opened
- Control Panel pop-up description
- Start button

Notice in the figure that Lauren's desktop looks a little different than the desktop you saw demonstrated in the previous tasks. For example, you see a different background displayed—this is another feature that you can customize.

2 Click on **Control Panel**.

This opens the Control Panel window.

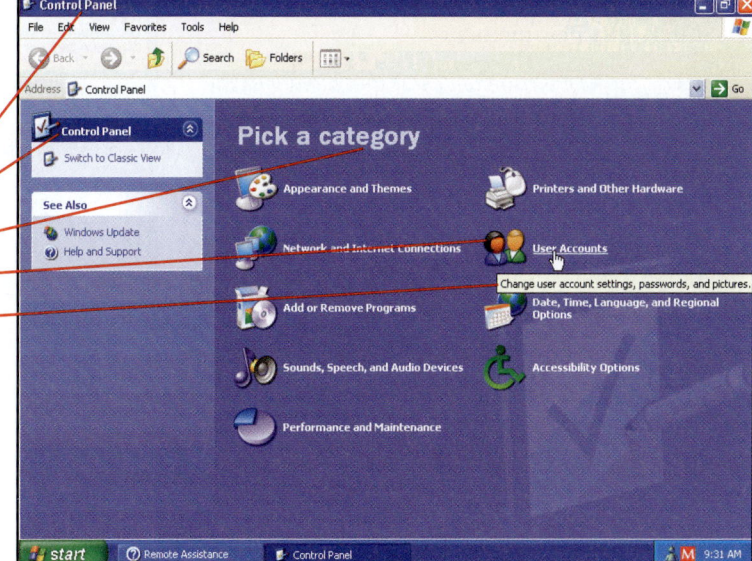

- Control Panel in title bar
- Left pane
- Pick a category in the right pane
- User Accounts category highlighted
- Pop-up description

Do not make any changes to your account unless you have permission.

Task 6   Changing Your User's Options   WIN   **19**

3 Click the **User Accounts** category in the right pane.

This opens the User Accounts window. Notice that very few tasks can be changed when you are logged in on a **limited account**, *which does not have administrator privileges. Windows XP provides both computer administrator and limited* **account types**. *A* **computer administrator account** *controls and maintains systems such as your computer. Your account is most likely a limited account.*

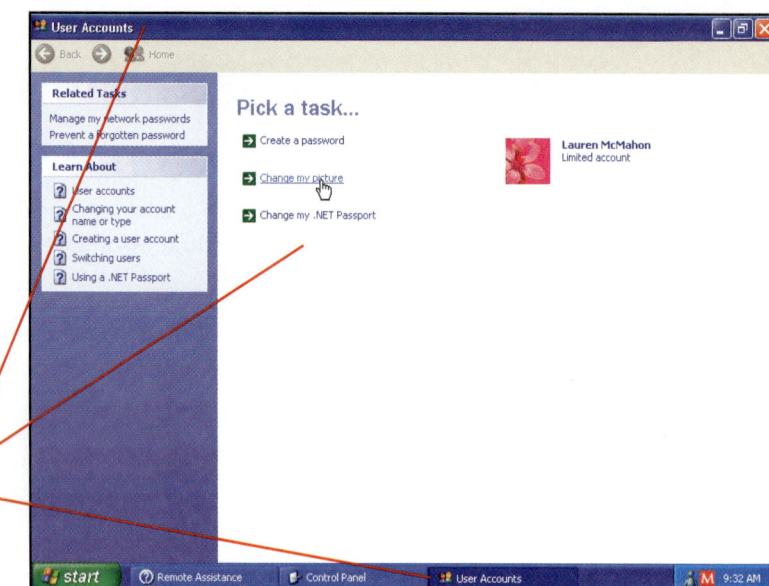

User Accounts window
Lauren's user account tasks
User Accounts button in taskbar

> **CAUTION**
> Although you can add a password to your own account, do not make such a change unless you have permission. Adding a password to an account used by multiple users will lock the others out of that account unless they too know the new password.

4 Click on **Change My Picture**.

This displays several pictures from which you can choose for your user account.

   Click on a new picture.

This selects the new picture you chose and highlights the Change Picture button.

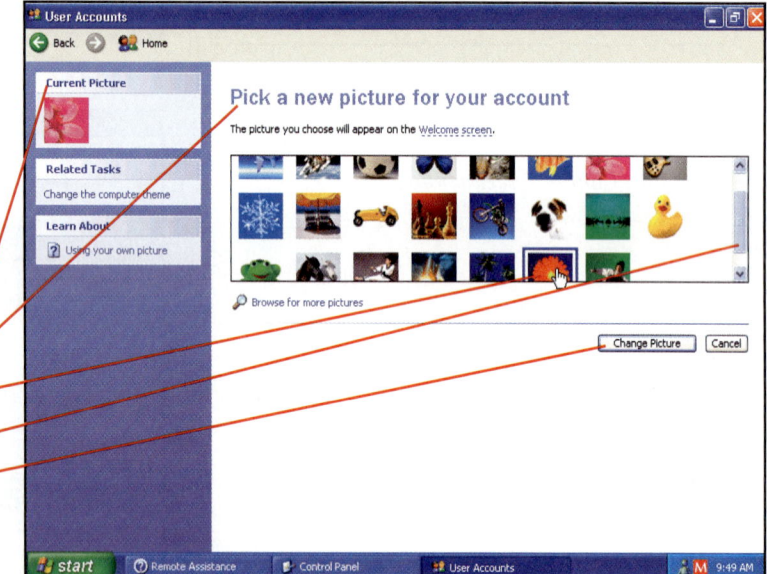

Current Picture section
Pick a new picture for your account window
Red flower selected
Scroll bar
Change Picture button

> **QUICK TIP**
> Notice the scroll bar to the right of the new picture choices. Use it by clicking and dragging it up or down to see the additional pictures available to you.

20   WIN   Lesson 1   Getting Started with Windows XP

 Click <u>C</u>hange Picture.

This applies the new picture you chose and returns you to the Pick a task window.

Pick a task window
Newly applied picture

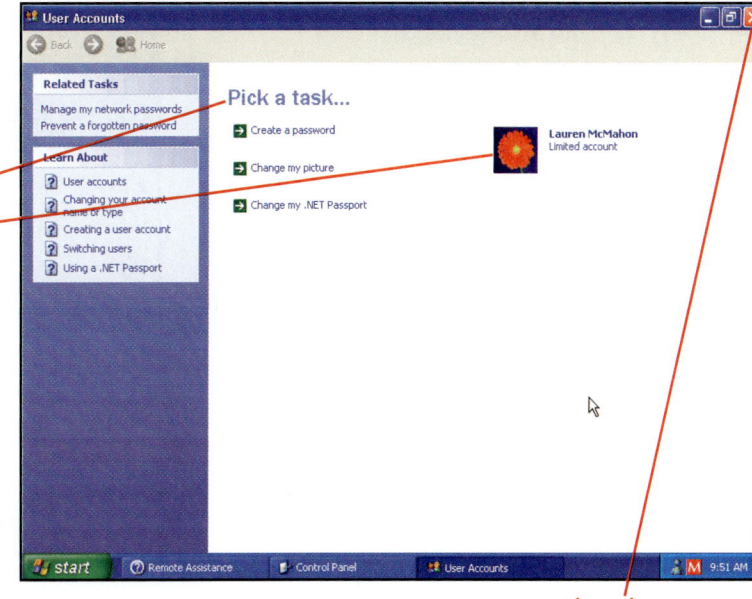

Close button

 Click the Close button.

This closes the Pick a task window.

Click the Close button.

This closes the Pick a category window and returns you to the desktop.

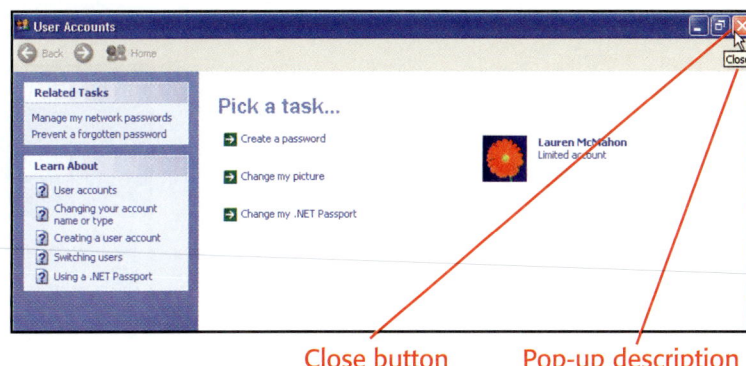

Close button   Pop-up description

Remember you can use one of the other methods for closing either of these windows, such as selecting the File option in the menu bar, and then clicking on Close.

Task 7
LOGGING OFF WINDOWS XP

Why would I do this?
Eventually you will finish all the tasks you have planned to accomplish in a work session. While logged into your Windows XP workstation, you have been in a secure environment where the operating system lets you accomplish tasks based on the *administrative rights* assigned to your user. When leaving your workstation you should *log off* the computer to end your session, and return it to the point where the next user must go through the logon procedures.

In this task, you learn how to log off Windows XP.

Task 7   Logging Off Windows XP   WIN   21

❶ Press 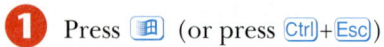 (or press Ctrl+Esc).

This opens the Start menu.

Point to the **Log Off** button.

This opens a pop-up description box explaining the uses of the Log Off button.

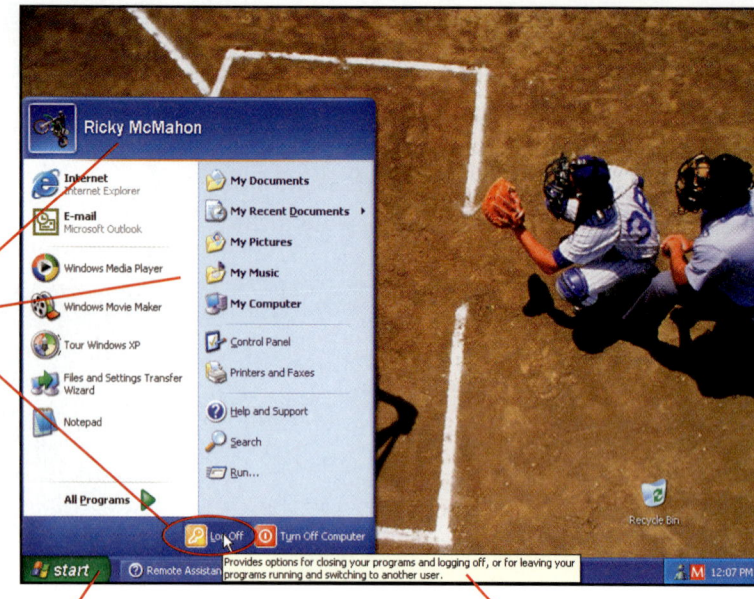

Ricky's user information
Start menu opened
Log Off button

Start button
Pop-up description

QUICK TIP

Notice the underlined "L" in the Log Off button's name. This appears when the Start menu is opened with 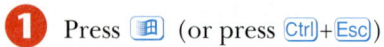 as opposed to clicking on the Start button. With the Start menu open, you can press L to select the Log Off option. You can also use this method to choose other items with underlined letters on the Start menu.

❷ Point to the **Turn Off Computer** button.

This opens a pop-up description box explaining the uses of the Turn Off Computer button.

Pop-up description
Turn Off Computer button

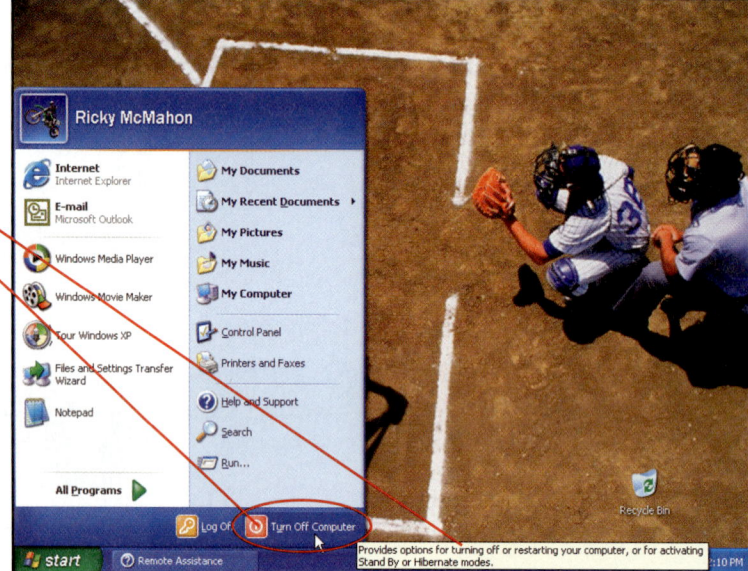

CAUTION

If you or your administrator has customized your workstation and named the computer, your Shut Down Computer button will insert that customized name in the place of "Computer." For instance, if my computer's name is "Rich's Workbox," then the button will show Shut Down Rich's Workbox.

22　WIN　Lesson 1　Getting Started with Windows XP

❸ Click the **Log Off** button.

This opens the Log Off Windows dialog box.

Point to the **Switch User** button.

This opens a pop-up description box explaining the effects of clicking the Switch User button.

Faded desktop
Log Off Windows dialog box

QUICK TIP
Note the information given at the bottom of the pop-up description. Pressing the (Windows logo key) + Ⓛ allows you to change users if your computer is a non-networked workstation. If it is a networked workstation, this same key combination locks the workstation, and only the person who locked it or the administrator will be able to unlock it for subsequent use.

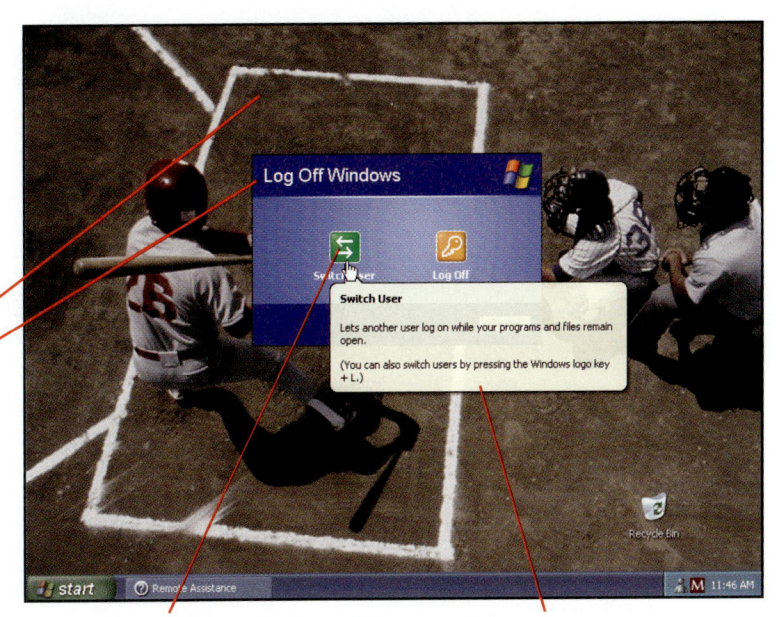

Switch User button   Pop-up description

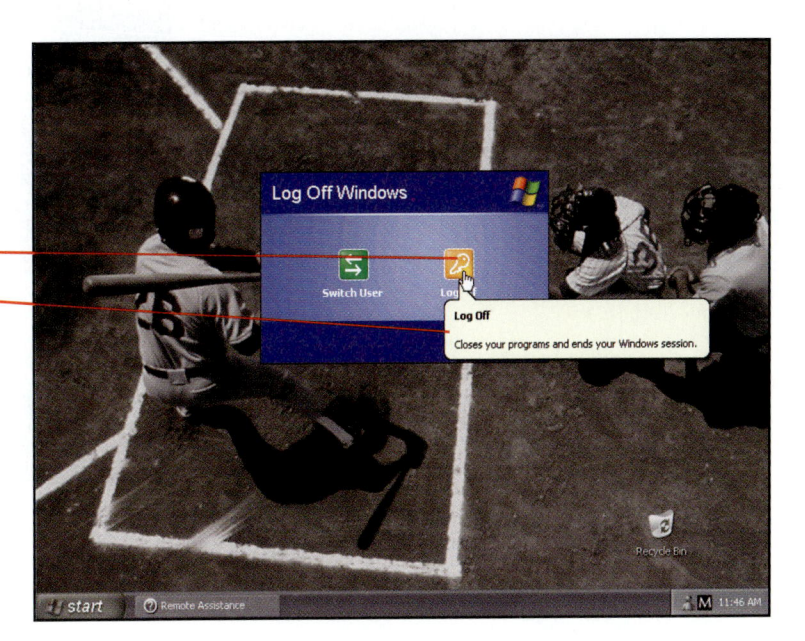

CAUTION
Having too many users working active applications on the computer through use of the Switch User function can degrade the workstation's operational capabilities.

❹ Point to the **Log Off** button.

This opens the pop-up description box explaining the effect of clicking the Log Off button.

Log Off button
Pop-up description

Task 7 Logging Off Windows XP WIN **23**

5 Click the Switch User button.

The Windows Welcome screen displays.

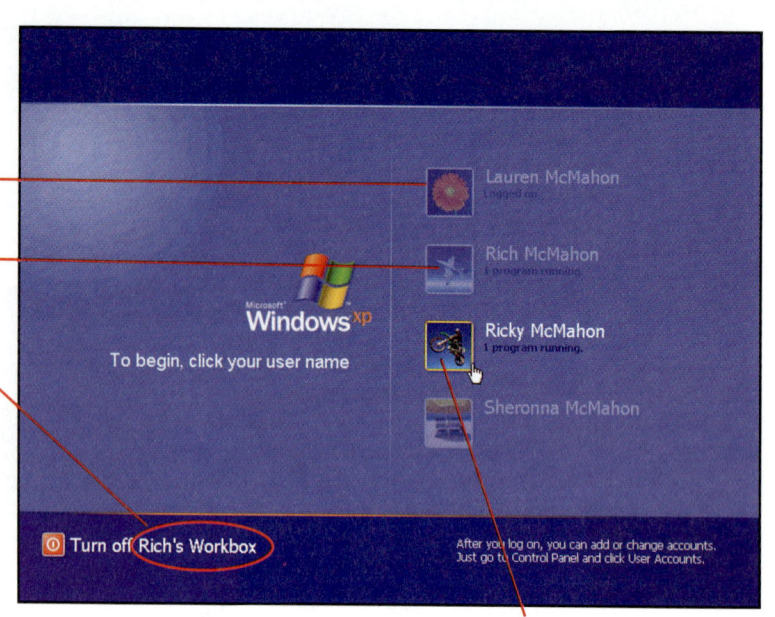

- Dimmed Lauren's user (logged on with no programs running)
- Dimmed Rich's user (logged on with one program running)
- Customized computer name
- Highlighted Ricky's user (logged on with one program running)

> **QUICK TIP**
>
> The **Switch User option** is a convenient way of leaving your current applications or opened objects in their current state while you allow another user (who is also authorized on that workstation) to log on to the workstation. When that other user is finished, you can immediately return to those already-opened objects. Although only one person can actually be working the desktop at a time, this Switch User feature allows multiple users to have work proceeding in the background.

6 Click the Turn Off Computer button.

This opens the Turn off computer dialog box.

- Turn off computer dialog box
- Hibernate button
- Turn Off button
- Restart button
- Turn Off Computer (or customized name) button

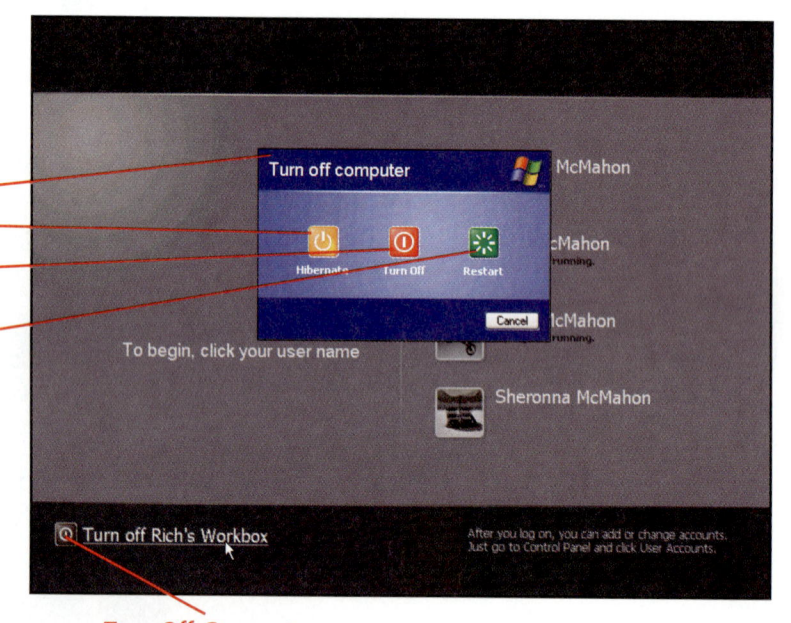

> **CAUTION**
>
> If you or your administrator has customized your workstation and named the computer, your Turn Off Computer button will insert that customized name in the place of "Computer." For instance, if my computer's name is "Rich's Workbox," then the button will show Turn Off Rich's Workbox.

7 Point to the **Hibernate** button.

This displays a pop-up description explaining the uses of the Hibernate feature. (If you are using a laptop computer, the button will be labeled Stand By instead of Hibernate, and will serve basically the same function.)

Hibernate button

Pop-up description

IN DEPTH

As the pop-up description states, clicking the Hibernate button allows you to save all your current settings to the hard disk and shut down the computer. The benefit of **hibernation** is that when you return, restarting your computer is very fast and returns you to the exact state you were in when you put the computer in the hibernate mode.

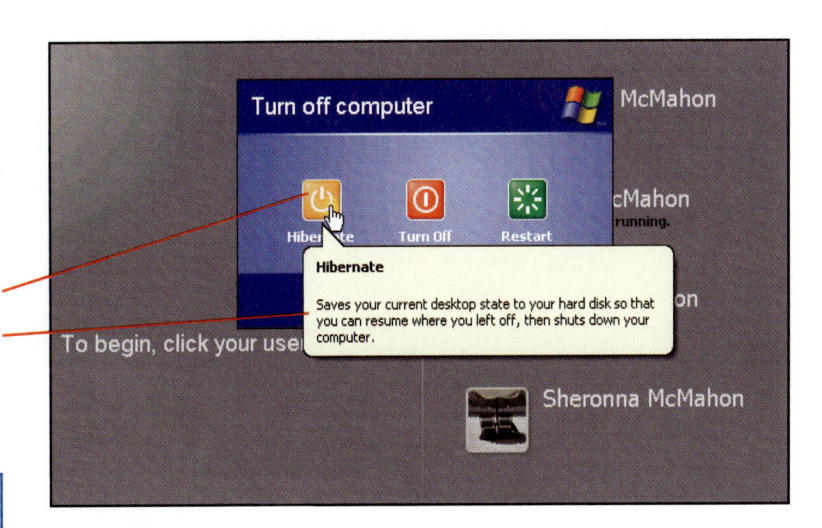

CAUTION

Do not click Hibernate on your computer unless you have permission. Doing so may terminate any work currently in progress by other properly logged-on users.

8 Point to the **Turn Off** button.

This displays a pop-up description explaining the uses of the Turn Off option.

Turn Off button

Pop-up description

CAUTION

Do not click the Turn Off button on your computer unless you have permission. Doing so will terminate any work currently in progress by other properly logged on users and any unsaved operations will be lost.

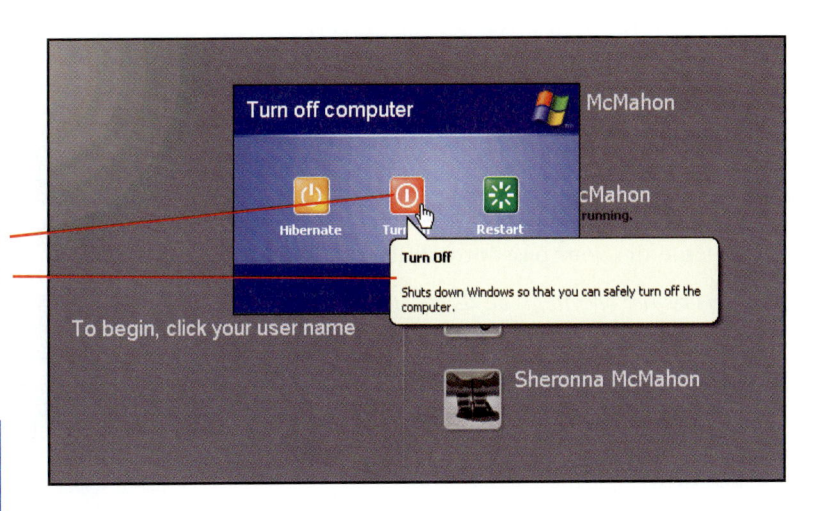

IN DEPTH

To properly shut down any Windows workstation, you must go through a shut-down procedure during which the operating system closes all of its open files and discards any temporary working items it has been using up to the point of shut down. Using this Turn Off button allows Windows XP to perform this procedure and properly shut down your workstation.

Task 7   Logging Off Windows XP   WIN   **25**

9 Point to the **Restart** button.

This displays a pop-up description explaining the uses of the Restart option.

Restart button
Pop-up description

IN DEPTH
Using this Restart button allows Windows XP to perform the required procedure and properly shut down your workstation prior to restarting.

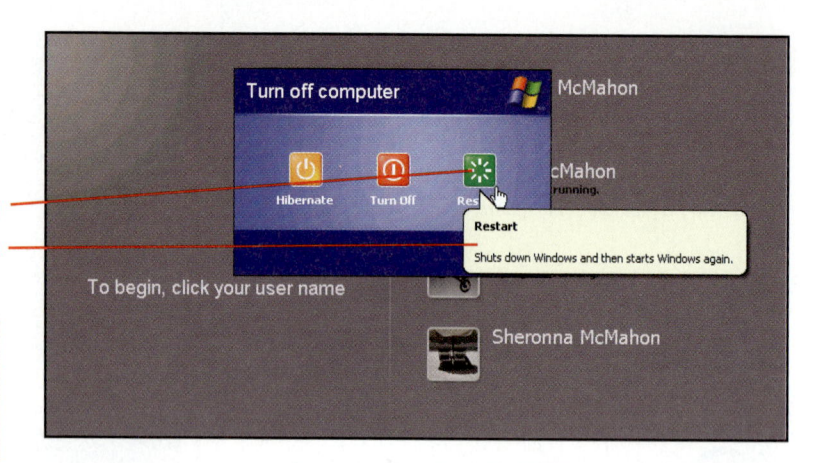

CAUTION
Do not click the Restart button on your computer unless you have permission. Doing so will terminate any work currently in progress by other properly logged-on users and any unsaved operations will be lost.

User's desktop dimmed

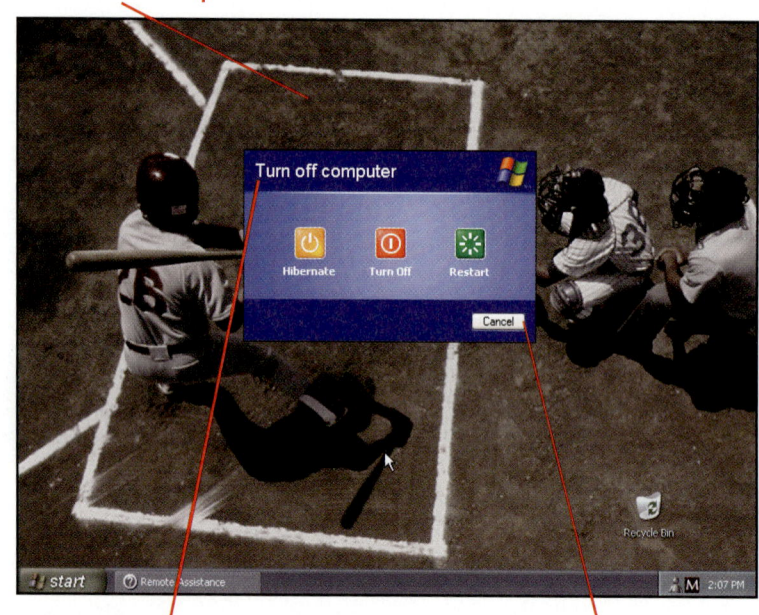

10 Click the **Cancel** button in the Turn off computer dialog box.

This cancels you out of the Turn off computer dialog box and puts you back at the Windows Welcome screen.

Click your user picture or your user name, then enter your password, if necessary.

You now resume operations on the desktop of your workstation because you are still shown as logged in.

Click the **Start** button, and then click the **Turn Off Computer** button.

This displays the Turn off computer dialog box. This is the same dialog box that was displayed when you clicked the Turn off computer button from the Windows Welcome screen.

Turn off computer dialog box   Cancel button

CAUTION
Do not click the Hibernate, Turn Off, or Restart buttons on your computer unless you have permission. Doing so will terminate any work currently in progress by other properly logged-on users and any unsaved operations will be lost.

26   WIN   Lesson 1   Getting Started with Windows XP

11 Click the Turn off computer dialog box's **Cancel** button.

This cancels you out of the Turn off computer dialog box and returns you to your desktop.

Click the **Start** button, and then click the **Log Off** button.

This opens the Log Off Windows dialog box.

Click the **Log Off** button.

This logs you off Windows XP and returns your workstation to the Windows Welcome screen for the next user to log on.

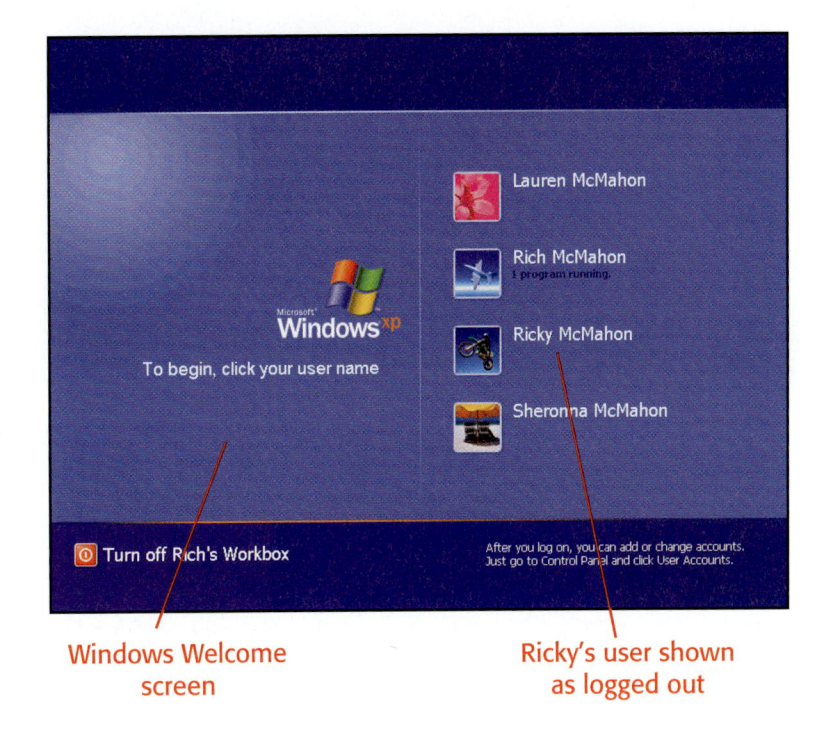

Windows Welcome screen

Ricky's user shown as logged out

Task 7   Logging Off Windows XP   WIN   27

The exercises that follow are designed for you to review and use what you have learned in this lesson. You also have the opportunity to practice your skills and then expand on them by applying them to new situations.

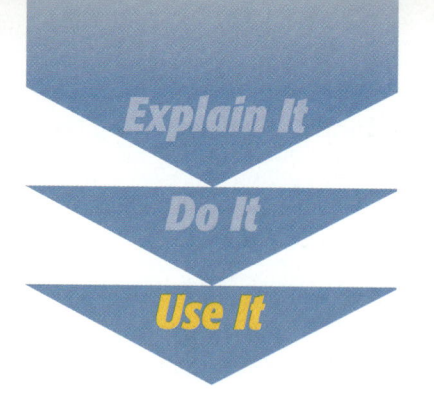

Explain It

Do It

Use It

COMPREHENSION

Comprehension exercises are designed to check your memory and understanding of the basic concepts in this lesson. You distinguish between true and false statements, identify new screen elements, and match terms with related statements. If you are uncertain of the correct answer, refer to the task number following each item (for example, T4 refers to Task 4) and review that task until you are confident that you can provide a correct response.

TRUE-FALSE

Circle either T or F.

T F 1. If you verify that your monitor is turned on and you still cannot see the default screen saver that your administrator implemented for you, a faulty monitor is most likely the cause. **(T1)**

T F 2. When passwords are entered during the Windows XP logon procedure, the individual characters are represented by an asterisk (*) so no casual observer can view them and obtain the password for later use. **(T1)**

T F 3. The Display pointer trails option is turned off by default. **(T2)**

T F 4. The sole purpose of the ⊞ key is to open your Start menu. **(T3)**

T F 5. To add a new folder to your desktop, a handy procedure begins by right-clicking a blank area on the desktop. **(T5)**

T F 6. Hibernate is the feature that allows multiple users to log on to the same computer simultaneously without having to shut down each other's programs. **(T7)**

MATCHING QUESTIONS

A. Click   D. Esc
B. Tab⇆   E. Point
C. Global   F. Picture

Match the following statements to the word or phrase that is the best match from the list. Write the letter of the matching word or phrase in the space provided next to the number.

1. ____ Point to an object, and then press and release the left mouse button. This action is often used to select an object or to place a cursor in the intended location. **(T2)**

2. ____ The key pressed to disregard all you entered when you make a mistake while naming a folder. **(T5)**

3. ____ The tab on the Recycle Bin Properties dialog box where settings are changed regarding trash emptying warnings. **(T4)**

4. ____ One of the customizable features users can likely change on their own user account. **(T6)**

5. ____ An action you can take on an object to make its pop-up description box display. **(T2)**

6. ____ The key pressed as an alternate means of navigating within dialog boxes and windows instead of using mouse clicks. **(T3)**

IDENTIFYING PARTS OF THE SCREEN

Refer to the figure and identify the numbered parts of the screen. Write the letter of the correct label in the space next to the number.

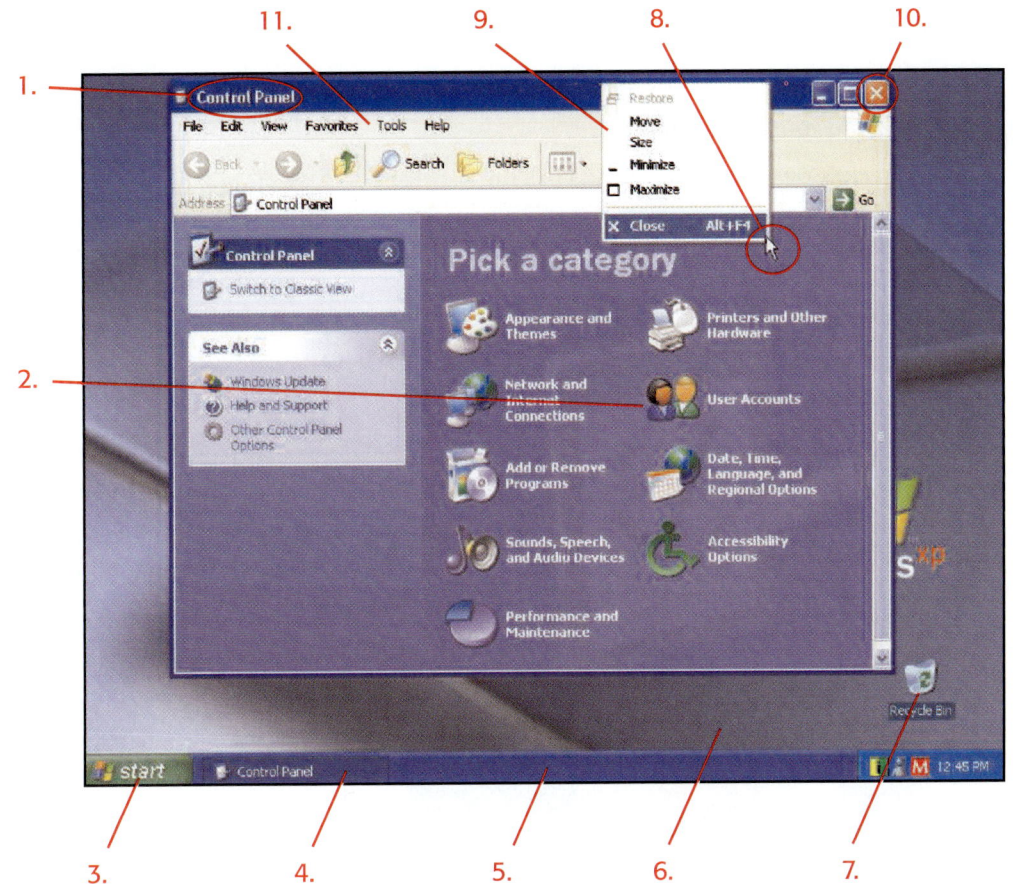

1. _____
2. _____
3. _____
4. _____
5. _____
6. _____
7. _____
8. _____
9. _____
10. _____
11. _____

A. Desktop (T1)

B. Shortcut menu (T2)

C. Start button (T2)

D. Menu bar (T1)

E. Name in title bar (T5)

F. Recycle Bin (T2)

G. Close button (T5)

H. User Accounts icon (T5)

I. Taskbar (T3)

J. Taskbar button (T3)

K. Mouse pointer (T1)

Comprehension   WIN   29

REINFORCEMENT

Reinforcement exercises are designed to reinforce the skills you learned by applying them to new situations. Detailed instructions are provided along with a figure, where appropriate, to illustrate the result. Complete the following reinforcement exercises sequentially.

R1—Changing the Default Screen Saver

1. Log on to your local computer.
2. Right-click on your desktop and click on **Properties**.
3. Click the **Screen Saver** tab of the Display Properties dialog box. This dialog box enables you to change what you see on your monitor.
4. Click the **Screen Saver** drop-down list in the middle of the dialog box.
5. Select **My Pictures Slideshow** from among the choices.
6. If you have permission to make changes on your workstation, click the **OK** button to apply the new setting and close the dialog box. Otherwise, click **Cancel**.

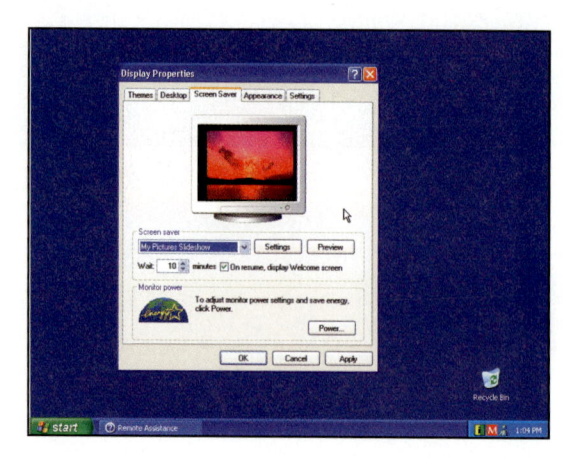

R2—Creating and Logging on with a New User Account

1. Log on to your local computer as a computer administrator user. (If you are not allowed to log on with this account type, you will be unable to perform this exercise.)
2. Click the **Start** button, then click **Control Panel**.
3. Click on **User Accounts**, then click on **Create a new account**.
4. Type **NEW ACCOUNT** as the name for the new account, and click the **Next** button.
5. Select the **Limited** option button as the type of account, and then click the **Create Account** button.
6. Click the newly created **NEW ACCOUNT** user.
7. Click **Create a password**. Enter and confirm **PASSWORD** as the password for the new account.
8. Enter **HINT** as the password hint, and then click the **Create Password** button.
9. Click **Delete the account**, and then click the **Delete Files** button.
10. Click the **Delete Account** button. Click the **Close** button twice to return to the desktop.

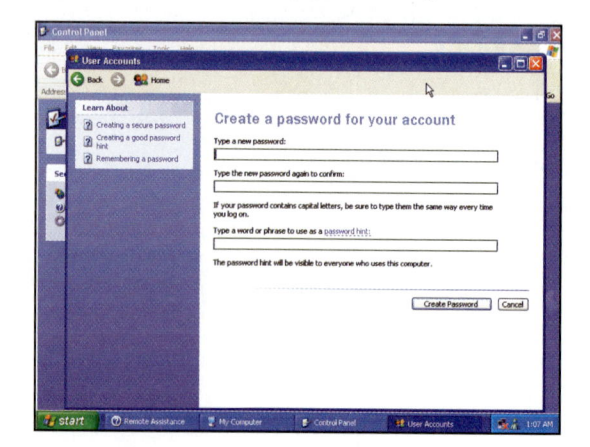

R3—Changing the Switch User Option

1. Log on to your local computer as a computer administrator user with no other users logged on to the workstation.
2. Click the **Start** button, and then click **Control Panel**.
3. Click on **User Accounts**, and then click on **Change the way users log on or off**.
4. Click to remove the check mark next to **Use Fast User Switching**.
5. If you have permission to make changes on your workstation, click the **Apply Options** button; otherwise, click **Cancel**.
6. Click the **Close** button twice to return to the desktop.
7. Click the **Start** button, and log off your workstation. Then, log back on to your workstation.
8. If you clicked the **Apply Options** button in Step 5, repeat the steps necessary to select the **Use Fast User Switching** check box and save your change.

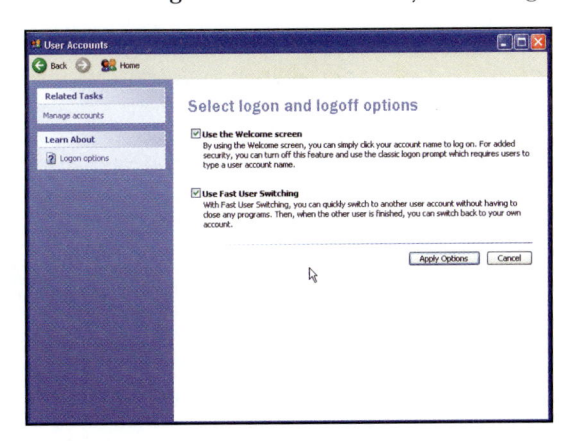

R4—Hibernating and Restarting a Workstation

1. Log on to your local computer as a computer with no other users logged on to the workstation.
2. Click the **Start** button, and then click **Turn Off Computer**.
3. If you have permission to make workstation changes, click on **Hibernate**; otherwise, complete this exercise by clicking **Cancel**.
4. Turn off your computer when your screen says, "**It is safe to turn off your computer.**"
5. Restart your computer and note that your user name is still shown as logged on.
6. Log back on under your user name. Notice that the restart is almost instantaneous, and the normal setup does not occur.

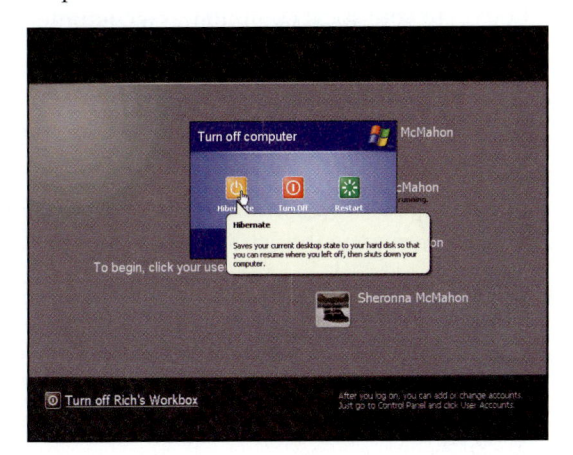

Reinforcement WIN 31

CHALLENGE

Challenge exercises are designed to test your ability to apply your skills to new situations with less-detailed instructions. These exercises also challenge you to expand your repertoire of skills by using commands that are similar to those you already learned. The desired outcome is clearly defined, but you have more freedom to choose the steps needed to achieve the required result.

C1—Customizing a New User Account

In this lesson, you worked with your own user account. That user account was given to you and was already created by someone else ahead of time. You also changed some of the typical user account settings. Now, in this challenge exercise, you create a new user account and customize some of that account's settings before deleting the account.

Goal: To create a user account and customize its settings.

1. Log on to your local computer as a computer administrator user.

2. Open the Control Panel and create a new account (for a new user named *Ezra Oriadha*) using the **Computer administrator** account type.

3. Click on Ezra's new account in the User Accounts window to change the settings.

4. Change the picture associated with Ezra's new account.

5. Change the name displayed on Ezra's account.

6. Add a password and a password hint to the account.

7. Change the new account's type to **Limited**.

8. Delete the new user account you just created, to prevent your local computer from becoming overloaded with unnecessary user accounts.

9. Click the Close buttons on both the User Accounts and Control Panel windows to close them and put you back on the desktop.

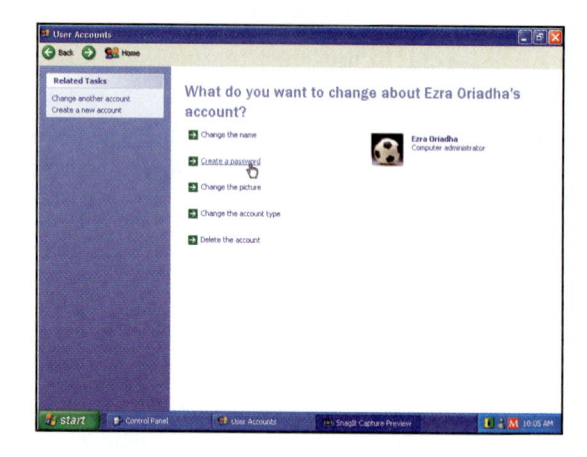

C2—Changing the Monitor's Power Option

You have seen the use of screen savers and have worked with the default screen saver setting (or what someone else changed the default to) already configured. There are many additional settings available for setting up the monitor and customizing it to your liking.

Goal: To learn how to further customize the monitor's settings.

1. Log on to your local computer.

2. Right-click on your desktop, click **Properties** in the shortcut menu, and then click the **Screen Saver** tab.

3. Click the P**o**wer button in the **Monitor power** section. The Power Options Properties dialog box displays.

4. In the P**o**wer schemes drop-down list on the **Power Schemes** tab, select the **Home/Office Desk** setting.

5. Click the **Turn off monitor** drop-down list and change the setting to After 5 mins.

6. If you have permission to change your computer settings, click **OK** to apply the change and close the Power Options Properties dialog box. Otherwise, click the **Cancel** button to disregard your changes.

7. Click the **Close** button on the Display Properties dialog box to return to the desktop. If you had permission to apply them, you can verify your new settings by viewing the monitor for the time you set above and ensuring the monitor does power down after that period of time.

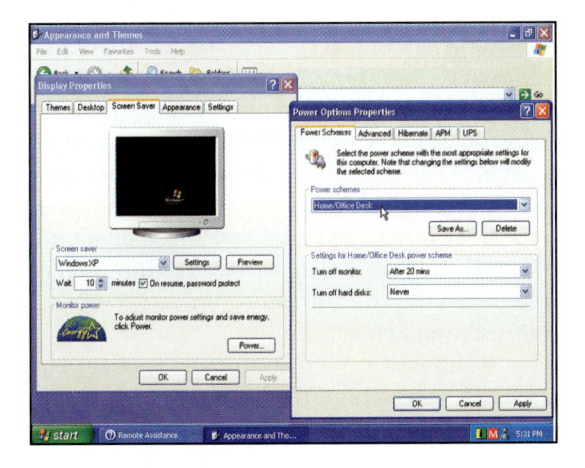

> **QUICK TIP**
> You also can access the Notepad application via the Accessories menu in Windows XP. Click the Start button, point to the All Programs option, point to Accessories, and then slide down to and click the Notepad item.

C3—Creating a New Folder and Text Document

In addition to creating folders and adding dummy files to occupy space, you should be able to work with simple text documents. Windows XP comes with such a text-based application already installed and ready for your use.

Goal: To create a new folder and a simple text document, and then save, print, and close the document.

1. Log on to your local computer.

2. Click the **Start** button and then click on **My Documents**.

3. Right-click in the center of the right pane (where the My Music and the My Pictures folder icons are), then select **New**, **Folder** to create a new folder.

4. While the name of the folder is still highlighted, type the new folder name, **Sample Documents**, and press ⏎Enter.

5. Double-click on your new **Sample Documents** folder to open it in a window.

6. Right-click inside that newly created and now-opened folder, select **New** (notice the additional types of new items you can create—Bitmap Image, Wave Sound, and so on), and then click on **Text Document**.

7. While the new item's name is still highlighted, type the new document's name as **Sample Document** and press ⏎Enter. Double-click that new document's icon to open a simple word-processing application called *Notepad*, which displays a blank text area.

8. Type the following inside the Notepad window:
   This is a simple text sentence that shows the capabilities of the Notepad word-processing application that comes preloaded inside my Microsoft Windows XP Professional computer.
   As you type, your pointer (commonly called the *insertion point*) turns into an "I"-beam character. The insertion point appears at the location where you begin adding the letters as you type them into your document.

9. To read the entire sentence, you may need to click and drag the scroll bar at the bottom of the Notepad window (between the left and right arrow buttons) as you read along the top line of text.

10. In the menu bar at the top of the Notepad window, click on **Format**, then select **Word Wrap**. Notice that the sentence you typed automatically fits within the confines of the window's edges and that you can read the entire sentence.

11. Choose **File**, **Save**. This saves the document with the text and formatting that you just entered above.

12. If your computer is connected to a printer, choose **File**, **Print** (otherwise, skip to Step 13). This displays the Print dialog box. To use the default settings to print one copy of the document to the current printer, click the **Print** button.

Challenge WIN 33

13. Click the Close button of the Notepad window. Double-click the text document's icon in the Sample Documents folder again to verify that the changes were made and saved to your document and then close the document again.

14. Click the Close button to close the Sample Documents folder and you should arrive at the My Documents folder.

15. Click the Close button to return to the desktop.

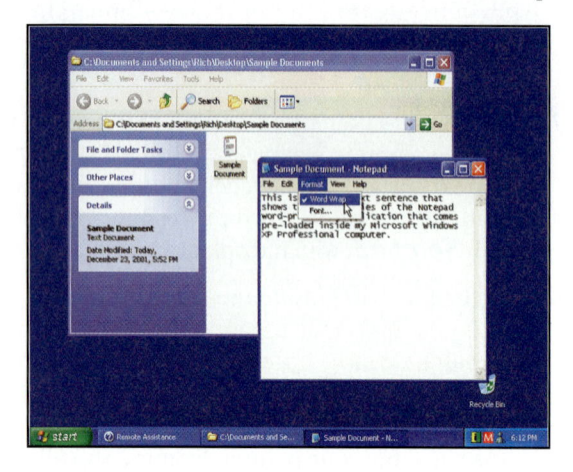

C4—Starting Your Browser and Navigating to a Web Site

In this lesson, you learned how to create files and folders. An additional feature of working with folders on your computer is that it closely resembles the structure of what is stored out on the Internet. Knowing how to work with files and folders in Windows XP makes it easier for you to find and work with objects on the Internet. This exercise requires a previously established *Internet connection*, a transmission path such as a phone line or network connection between your computer and the Internet.

Goal: To browse to and navigate a Web site.

1. Log on to your local computer.

2. Click the Start button, then click on your browser's icon at the top of the left frame (the default icon will be Microsoft's *Internet Explorer*, which is the browser that is used in the remainder of this text series). This action starts your Web browser.

3. If it is the first time the browser has started (although that is unlikely in a school or business setting), Microsoft has Internet Explorer ask that you specify your country and language being used, and then offers to help you designate its **www.MSN.com** as your *home page* (the Internet location where you start each time you open your browser). You should specify the country and language you will be using on your computer and then decide whether to use MSN.com as your home page. If you do, Microsoft will open that site for you when you accept the offer. If not, then you should specify a home page that you chose or set it to open to a blank page if want to save startup time each time you use your browser. You can always change this setting at a later time.

   If this is not the first time the browser has started, your school (or, on your home computer, this may be your software installer) has probably already set your home page for you. Either way, your browser will end up opening to the preselected Web site for you.

4. Click inside the white area in the address bar (the drop-down list near the top of the screen). The address will be highlighted for you and will be ready for you to type in a new address that you want your browser to find. When you enter Web site addresses, you must be exact with every character. Type **http://www.prenhall.com/**, and then press ↵Enter:

   This is Prentice Hall's Web site. Prentice Hall is the publisher of this text's series of *Windows XP Professional* books and many more educational items. The site is full of information and links for many of the publisher's book series.

5. Near the bottom of the Prentice Hall Web page, pass your mouse pointer over the item listed under **Resource Central**, labeled **Students**. Notice that it is underlined and that your pointer changes from an arrow to a hand pointing with its index finger. That change (and the tell-tale underline under the item) indicates that what appears to be just a word underlined for emphasis is actually what is referred to as a *hyperlink* (an item which, when clicked on, sends your browser to another corresponding Web page). In fact, if you slide your mouse pointer over it again, once the pointer changes to the hand, look in the lower left corner of your browser's window. There, next to the Internet Explorer icon (a small "e" on top of a dog-eared sheet of paper), you will see the actual Internet address displayed for that Web site. In this case, you should see the following link: **http://www.prenhall.com/resource_central/students/index.html**

6. Click the **Students** hyperlink and go to Resource Central's Students Web page. In the upper-right corner of the page, use the Discipline Finder pull-down box to locate information on this series of texts.

ON YOUR OWN

Microsoft maintains Web site locations that provide all the latest information regarding its operating systems. The newly released Windows XP Professional is no exception. The site's Internet address is: **http://www.microsoft.com/windowsxp/pro/**. Go there for information such as purchase evaluation assistance, product tours, software updates, comparisons between the different versions of XP, Windows XP "How to" articles, tips, downloads, and much more. In addition, this site is the best source for the latest articles discussing Windows XP.

Using the above site, simulate your intent to buy several new pieces of hardware for your computer at work, and search the site to find components compatible with Windows XP Professional. Start by using the site's Search window and begin your search with "Hardware Compatibility." From the list of related links, choose several that hint of an ability to help you choose products made expressly to work with Windows XP. (The site is updated frequently, so the search results may change from one day to the next.)

Use the links you find at this site to locate a new cordless optical mouse, ergonomically designed keyboard, laser color printer, flatscreen monitor, emergency backup software, uninterruptible power supply (UPS), digital camera, flatbed scanner, and virus protection program—all designed for Windows XP. Use Notepad to compile a detailed list of your proposed purchase. This list should include the item's name, part number, manufacturer, description, system requirements (if given), and price. You will have to go to the manufacturer's Web sites for prices and other equipment information. The Microsoft site normally links you to these sites. Print the list you created in Notepad, and then close Notepad without saving the file.

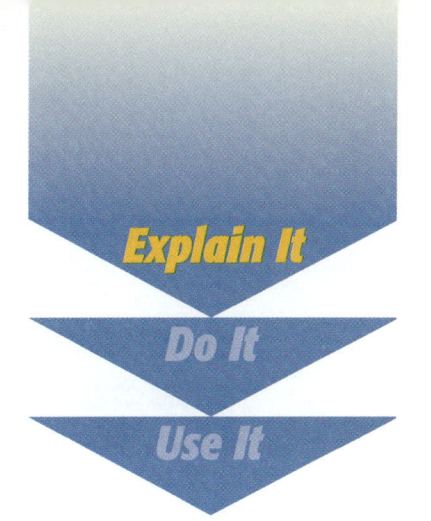

Lesson 2

Explain It
Do It
Use It

Working with Folders and Files

Task 1   Using File and Folder Navigation Tools
Task 2   Navigating to the My Documents Folder
Task 3   Switching to the Windows Explorer View
Task 4   Customizing the Start Menu
Task 5   Gathering Hard Drive Details
Task 6   Using the Search Feature
Task 7   Formatting a Floppy Disk
Task 8   Opening and Closing an Application

INTRODUCTION

Now that you have the basic foundation for working with Windows XP, you are ready to progress at a more rapid pace. To do this, you need to add the necessary framework upon which the remainder of your work with this operating system will heavily depend. This lesson takes the introductory foundations you learned in Lesson 1 and expands their use considerably.

We start by introducing you to many of the common file and folder navigation tools, and we discuss the preferred method for getting around inside Windows XP Professional—*Windows Explorer*. You also learn an alternative means of navigating Windows XP Professional—using *My Computer*. You examine the details of these features, and practice with the file and folder skills you developed in Lesson 1. In addition, we show you some of the handy shortcuts available to make your life easier as you navigate Windows XP Professional. Finally, you learn how to open and close *WordPad*, a word processing application included with Windows XP.

In this lesson, you learn how to navigate Windows XP Professional using two different techniques. You also learn how to use the computer's interface and alter some of the operating system's settings and options.

VISUAL SUMMARY

When you complete this lesson, you will have worked with a desktop that looks like this:

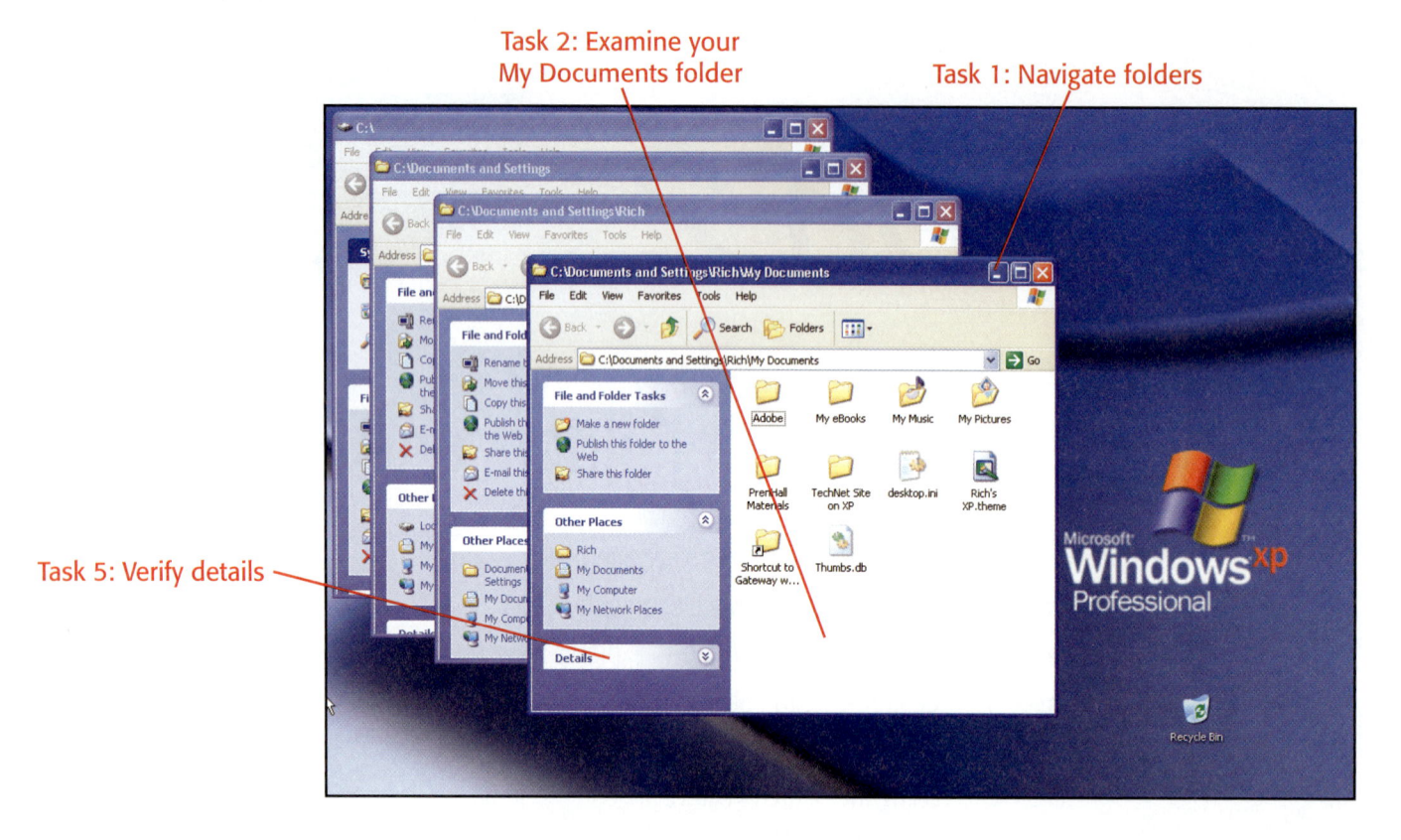

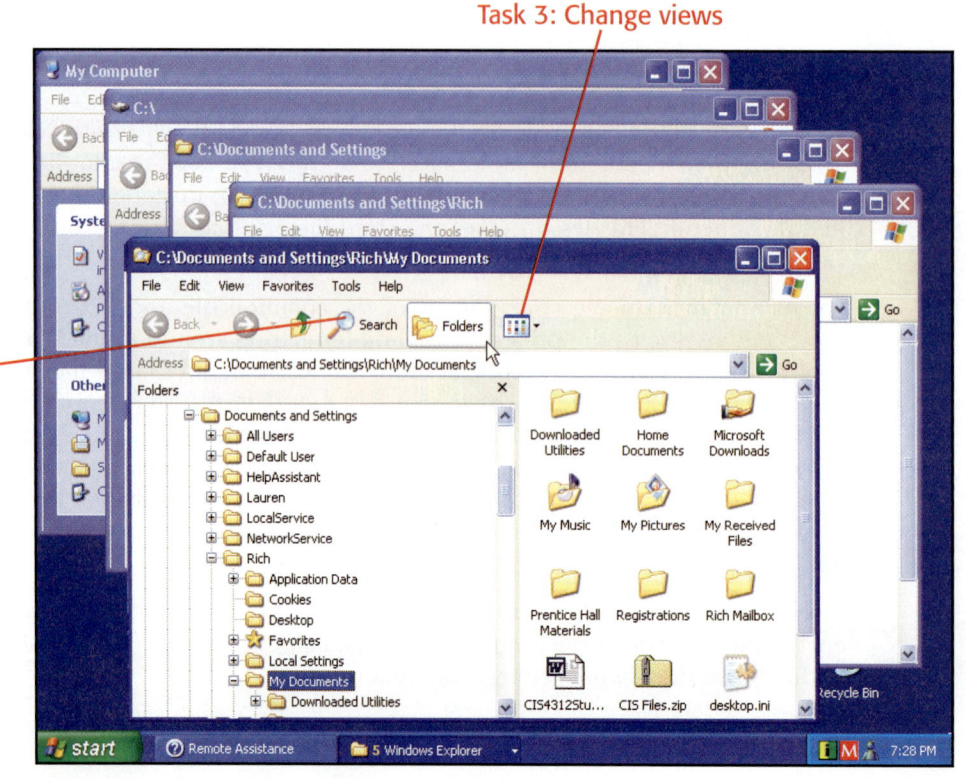

Task 2: Examine your My Documents folder

Task 1: Navigate folders

Task 5: Verify details

Task 3: Change views

Task 6: Search for an object

Task 1
USING FILE AND FOLDER NAVIGATION TOOLS

Why would I do this?
To use the file and folder skills you developed in Lesson 1 effectively, you must become more proficient with the tools available to you. Many of these tools are available to you in each window you create using Windows XP. Some of them are designed to help you organize and keep your workspace clutter-free.

Your desktop may appear different than the figures displayed in this and the following lessons, because the default settings and some of the customizable settings discussed in Lesson 1 have likely been changed by whoever maintains your computer. Such changes should have little effect on any of these lessons.

In this task, you learn to use the common tools available to you when working with files and folders.

1 Click the **Start** button.

This opens your Start menu.

Slide up to and click the **My Documents** icon.

The My Documents window opens. **My Documents** *is a default folder used for storing files, folders, or other objects. Notice the three buttons at the right end of the title bar (Minimize, Maximize/Restore, and Close).*

Title bar navigation buttons

Title bar
Taskbar button pressed

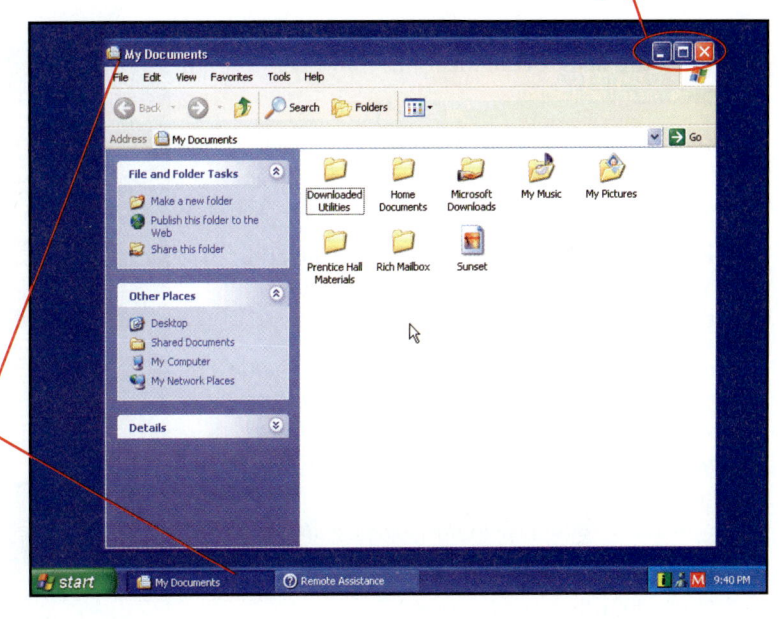

> **CAUTION**
> Your screen may not appear exactly as shown. First of all, it will not have the Remote Assistance button in the taskbar and the window may fill the entire desktop rather than partially filling it. At this point, whether or not it fills the screen does not make a difference. You could, however, click the Restore button (the middle of the three buttons on the title bar) to get your display more like the one used in this lesson. **Remote Assistance**, a new feature with this version of the Windows operating system, allows you to request help from someone and lets that individual take complete control of your computer from a remote location.

2 Click the title bar's **Minimize** button.

*The **Minimize button** reduces the object to a button on the taskbar. Its use is designed to help reduce clutter on your desktop. In this instance, clicking the Minimize button brings you to a clean desktop.*

Clean desktop
Taskbar button no longer pressed

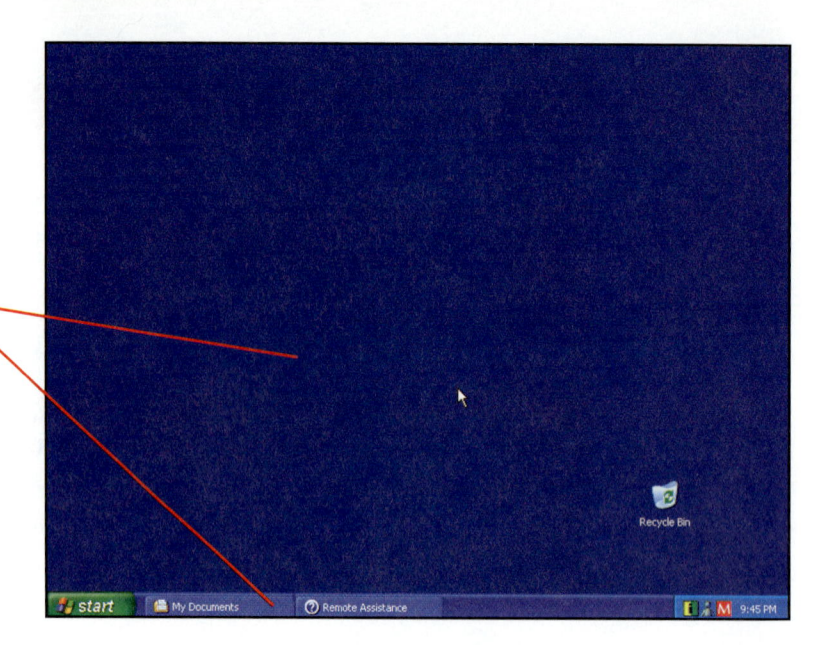

3 Click the **My Documents** button in the taskbar.

This once again opens the My Documents window. Note that it opens to the same size as it was before you clicked the Minimize button.

Point to (and pause on) and then click the **Maximize** button, the middle of the three title bar buttons.

*If, when you point to and pause on that middle button (often referred to as the **Maximize/Restore button**), its pop-up description reads **Restore Down** instead of **Maximize**, the window is already maximized and you can skip to the next paragraph. Clicking on the Maximize button opens the window to its maximum size (where it fills the desktop).*

Click the title bar's **Restore** button.

This resizes your window to the same dimensions as it was before you maximized it. Note that the Maximize button changes its name when the window is opened to its maximum size. It becomes the Restore button (actually, by pointing to and pausing over it with your mouse, you can see the pop-up description Restore Down).

Minimize, Maximize/Restore, and Close buttons

Pop-up description

QUICK TIP
Look closely at the Maximize button and compare it with the Restore button. The Maximize button has a single file in its icon and the Restore button has two files. This slight difference should help you when deciding if your window has simply been resized to fit the window or if it is maximized.

IN DEPTH
Another way to access the Minimize, Maximize/Restore, and Close functions is by pressing the [Alt] key and then the [Spacebar] to reveal the **Control menu** with its drop-down menu of those functions (and two additional items). As is typical with most Windows actions, you have numerous alternatives to accomplish the same task.

40 WIN *Lesson 2* Working with Folders and Files

4 Point to the right edge of your My Documents window.

This reveals a small double-headed arrow used to resize the windows horizontally.

Drag the double-headed arrow to the left, then release the mouse button.

This resizes your My Documents window and makes it smaller horizontally.

Doubled-headed resizing arrow

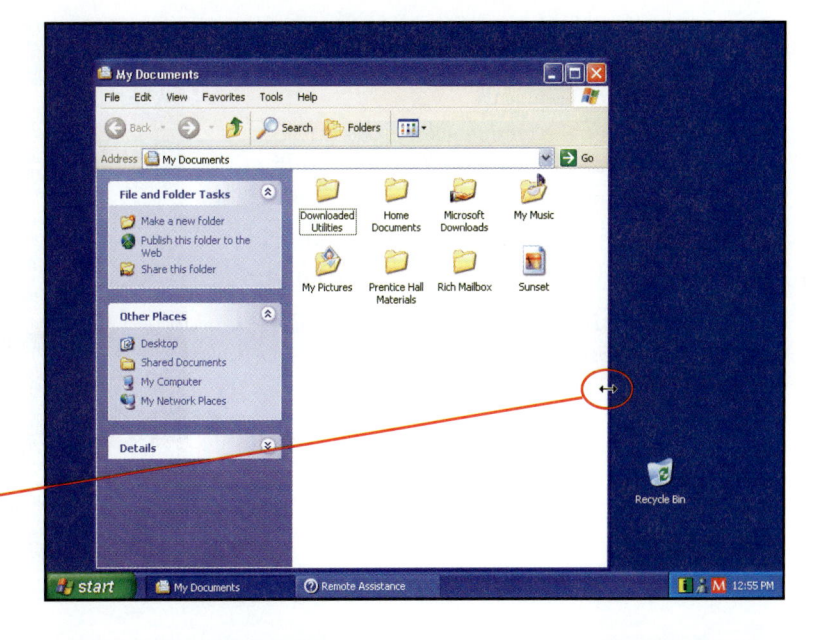

5 Point to the bottom edge of your My Documents window.

This reveals a small double-headed arrow used to resize the window vertically.

Drag the double-headed arrow up, then release the mouse button.

This resizes your My Documents window and makes it smaller vertically.

Double-headed resizing arrow

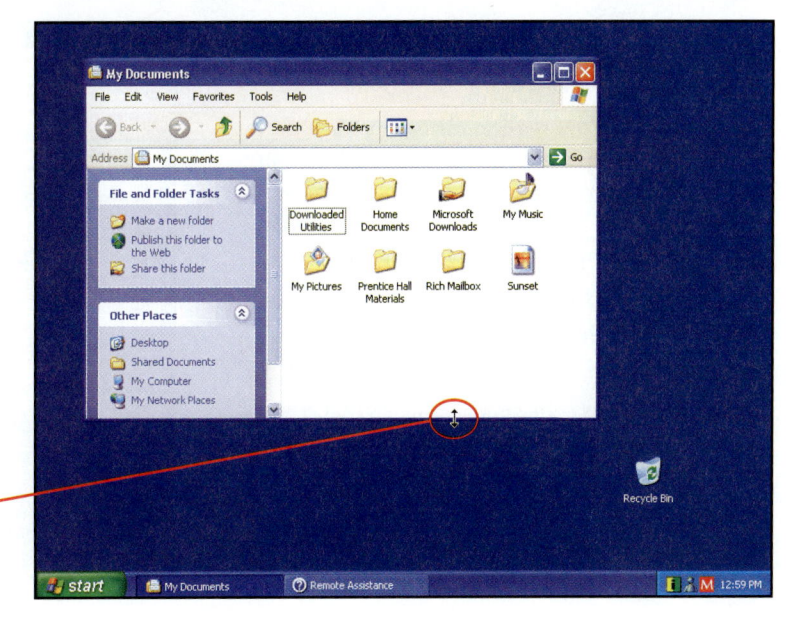

Task 1   Using File and Folder Navigation Tools   WIN

6 Point to the bottom-right corner edge of your My Documents window.

This reveals a small diagonal double-headed arrow used to resize the window horizontally and vertically at the same time.

Drag the double-headed arrow up and to the left, and then release the mouse button.

This resizes your My Documents window and makes it smaller both horizontally and vertically in one movement.

Double-headed resizing arrow

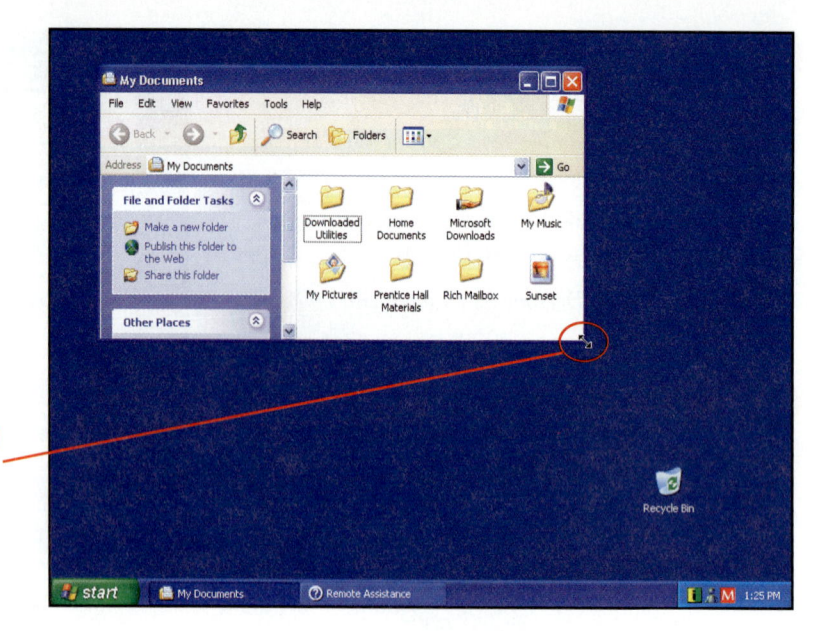

7 Click the **Views** button on the toolbar, then select **Thumbnails**.

*The **Views button** changes the view of the objects in your folder. Note that you may have to maximize your window to view the objects contained in your folder. Notice that in this case, there are five different views from which to choose. This number may vary depending on which folder you are viewing.*

Click the **Views** button again, then select **Icons**.

This returns you to the previous view.

Folder icon
Views button and choices

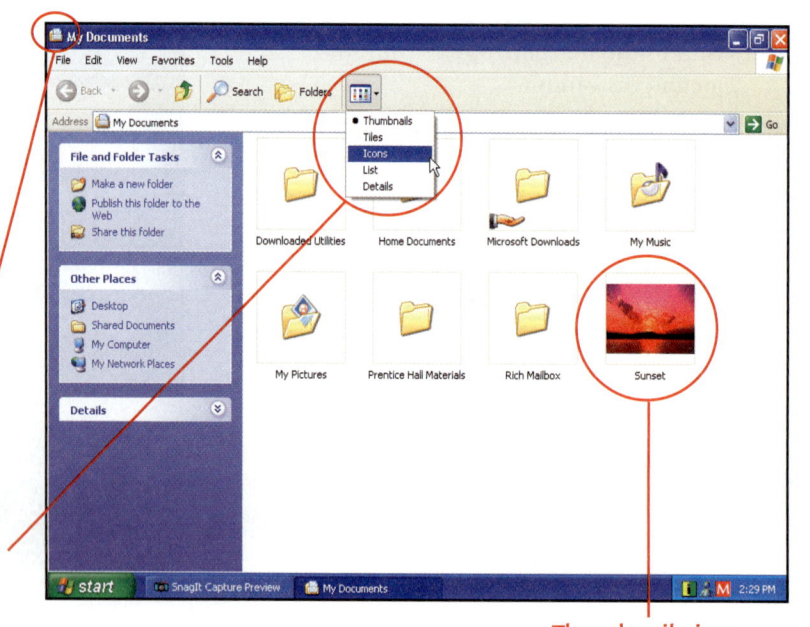

Thumbnail view of an object

8 Double-click the folder icon in the title bar's far-left corner.

*This is another way to activate the **Close** option. Double-clicking that icon closes your window and puts you back at your empty desktop.*

42　　WIN　　Lesson 2　　Working with Folders and Files

Task 2
NAVIGATING TO THE MY DOCUMENTS FOLDER

Why would I do this?
Sometimes you may have to navigate to an item's location inside your computer. You may not know exactly what the item is called, but you know where it is, or you may want to view multiple objects along the way to the item you end up opening.

In this task, you learn to navigate through your computer using My Computer.

1 Click the **Start** button.

This opens your Start menu.

    Slide up to and click the **My Computer** icon.

The My Computer window opens. Notice the left activity pane and the right pane displaying the objects that are currently located in the My Computer folder. If the default settings have not been changed, your windows will not be left open as you enter and leave successive windows (as in the example to follow). However, as demonstrated in Lesson 1, the default may have already been changed so that the windows are left open.

Left activity pane
Right pane organized in groups by type

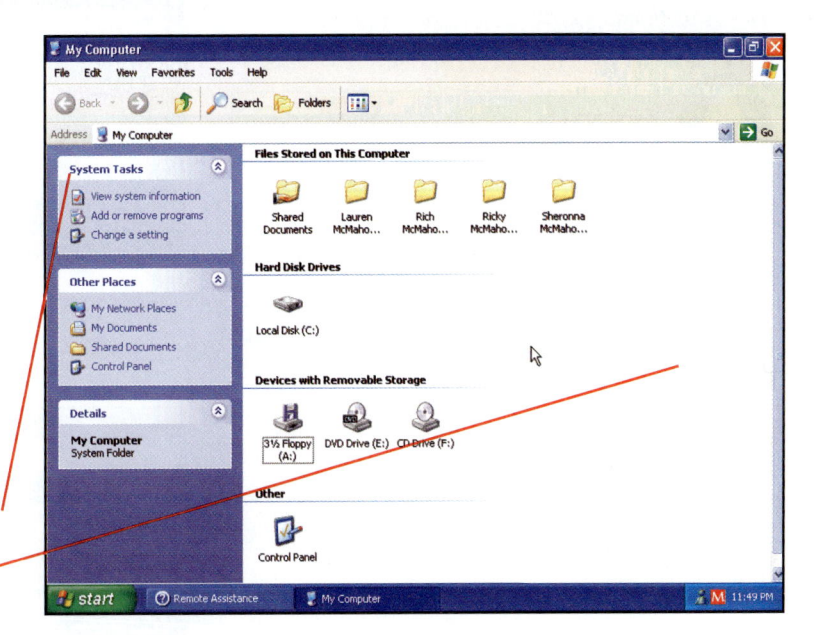

> **IN DEPTH**
> Notice that the items in the right pane are organized and grouped together by the object's type. For instance, the top section has the files all grouped together and the third section has the removable storage devices in another group. Your folder's settings may have your items displayed in another format. Their display at this point does not matter as long as you can still see that there are files stored there.

Task 2   Navigating to the My Documents Folder   WIN   **43**

2 Double-click the **hard disk drive** selection (**Local Disk C:** in this case).

This opens the hard disk drive (or hard drive), an internal component of your computer used for storage, so that you can review its contents.

Contents of Local Disk C: (the hard drive)

> **CAUTION**
> If you are not logged in as an administrator user, you may not be able to immediately access the C: drive files. You (and administrators with their accounts configured that way) will, instead, be warned that the system files are hidden. In the bottom of the right pane, however, simply click on **Show the contents of this folder** and it will still let you view the files.

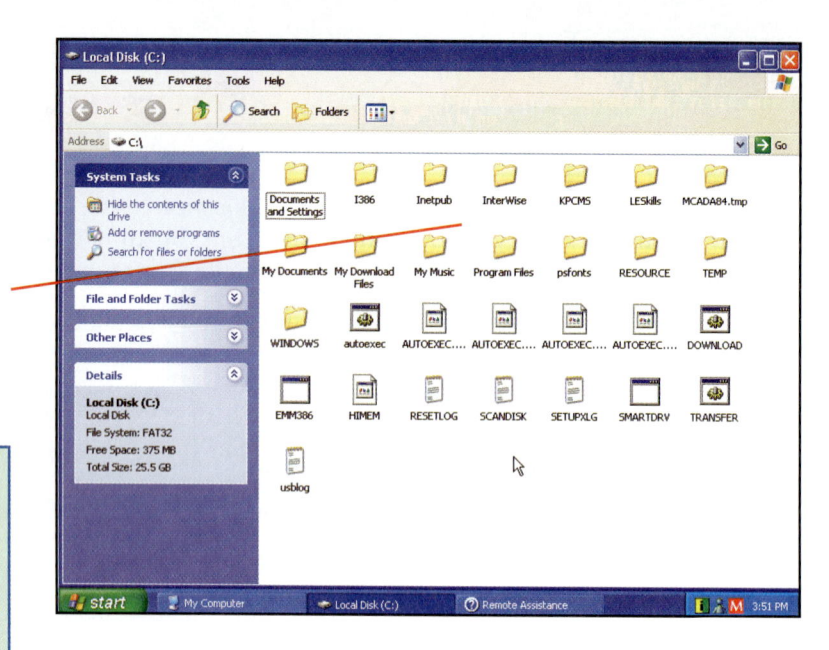

3 Double-click the **Documents and Settings** folder.

This displays the users with documents stored on your computer and any objects containing configuration settings.

Documents and Settings folder

Rich folder

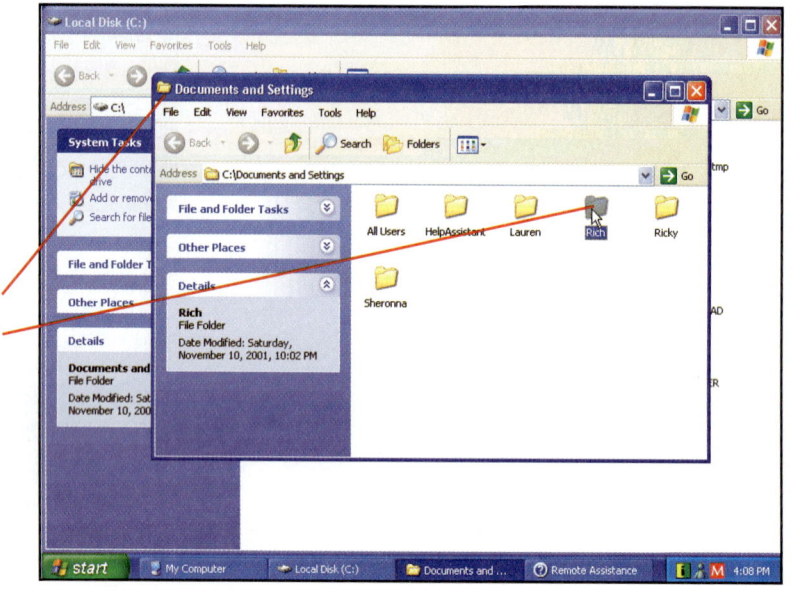

44   WIN   Lesson 2   Working with Folders and Files

4 Double-click the folder inside the Documents and Settings folder that has your user name (**Rich,** in this example).

Your folder opens and displays the files and folders you have stored in there.

Rich folder opened
Back and Forward arrows

> **QUICK TIP**
> If your computer is not configured to open all folders in separate windows, you can use the Back and Forward arrows to navigate back through the windows you have just opened and then return forward again to places you've already been.

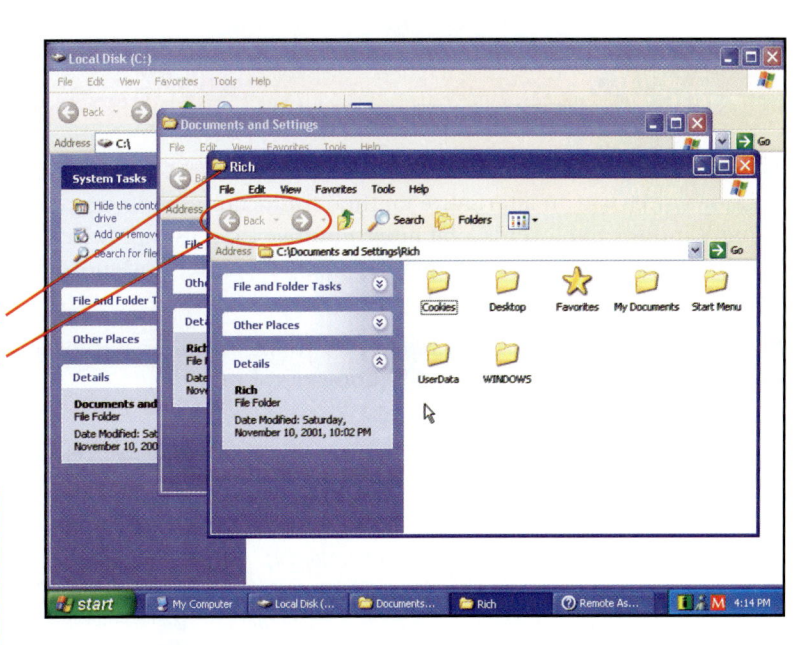

5 Double-click the **My Documents** folder.

This opens your My Documents folder and displays your user's stored objects.

> **CAUTION**
> Note that these documents may or may not all be yours if the user you signed on to Windows XP is shared between multiple individuals. Also notice that, unless security measures are implemented to prevent it (this is discussed in later lessons of this text series), the files you store in this folder are accessible to anyone who is allowed to log on to that workstation.

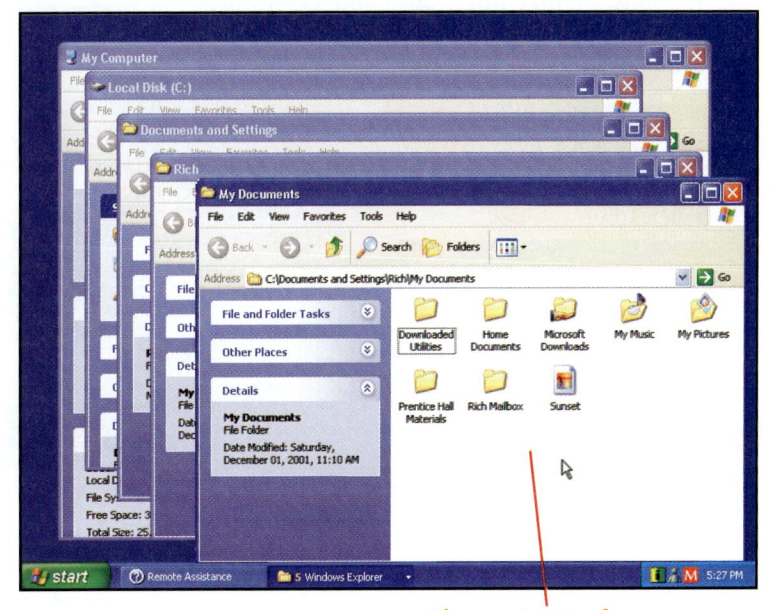

The contents of your My Documents folder

6 Right-click the **My Documents** button in the taskbar and select the **Close Group** (or **Close**) option.

This closes the entire group of five folders and returns you to the desktop. If the computer you use does not have folders opening in separate windows, you may see the Close option (rather than Close Group) when you right-click the taskbar button.

Task 2   Navigating to the My Documents Folder   WIN   45

Task 3
SWITCHING TO THE WINDOWS EXPLORER VIEW

Why would I do this?

Windows gives you an alternative method for locating items on your computer. Using Windows Explorer is a bit more intuitive than using My Computer. Also, you may find Windows Explorer somewhat easier to master and more likely to help you keep your desktop less cluttered.

In this task, you open a folder, switch over to the Windows Explorer view, and then navigate to the same folder using Windows Explorer.

1 Click the **Start** button, and then click the **My Documents** icon.

This opens the My Documents folder in a window. If the window is maximized, click the Restore button in the right corner of the window's title bar, and resize the window as indicated (if necessary).

Click the **Tools** menu, and select **Folder Options**. Change the Browse folders setting to **Open each folder in its own window**, and then click the **OK** button.

This changes the default folder browsing configuration such that each folder opens in a separate window.

Title bar
Maximize/Restore button
Action sidebar

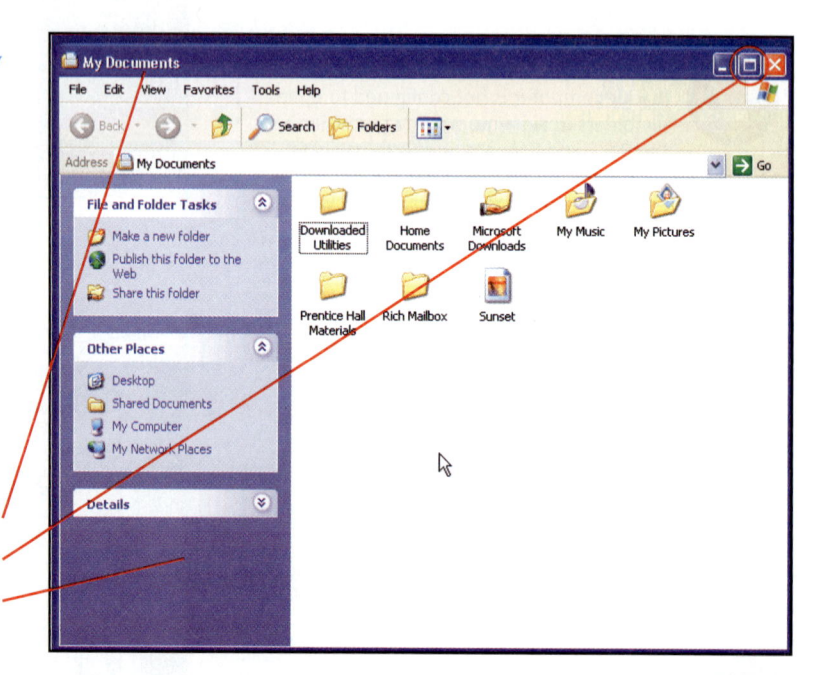

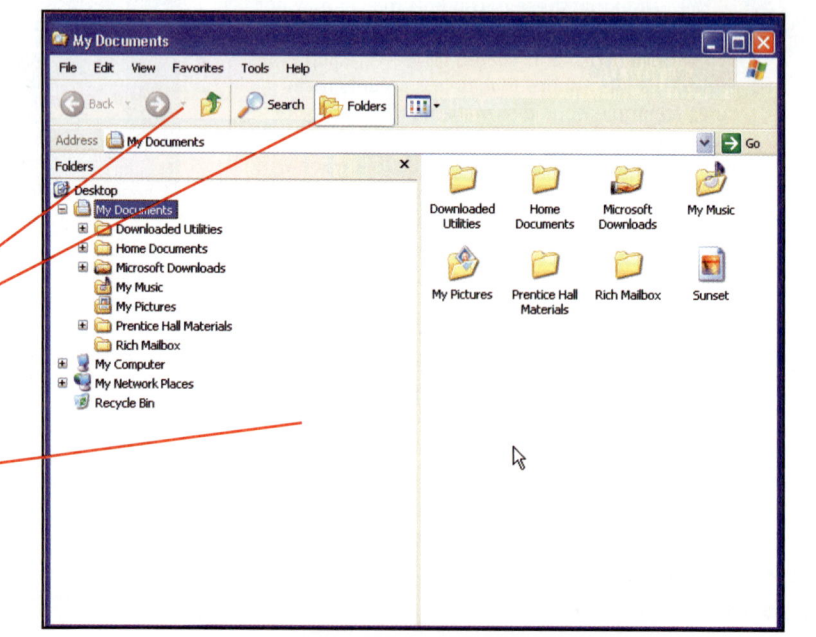

2 Click the **Folders** button in the toolbar.

You now see the Windows Explorer view. The Windows Explorer navigation pane has replaced the action sidebar on the left side of the window.

Toolbar buttons
Folders button

Windows Explorer navigation pane

46 WIN Lesson 2 Working with Folders and Files

❸ Click the **Folders** button in the toolbar again.

This returns you to the former My Computer navigation method, used in the My Documents window. Notice that the navigation pane is again replaced by the three context-sensitive areas in the action sidebar on the left. (Ignore any applications that are also opened, such as the Remote Assistance button shown in the illustration's taskbar.)

Click the **Start** button, and then click the **My Computer** icon.

This opens the My Computer window but still keeps your My Documents window open. Once again, make sure your windows are not maximized by clicking on the Restore button (if available) and resizing the window as necessary.

Current location in address bar

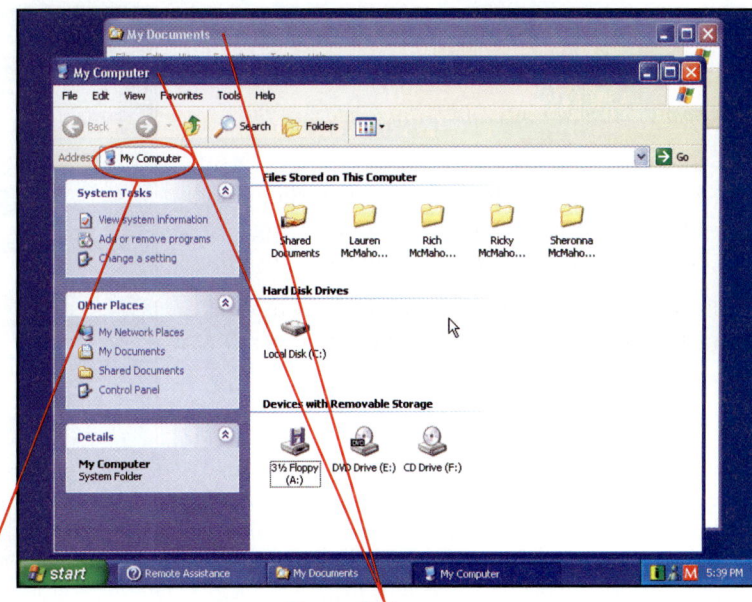

Two windows open

❹ Hold down the Ctrl key and double-click on **Local Disk C:**.

This opens your local hard drive. Notice that the C: folder has opened inside the same window where My Computer was opened, and that you still only have two windows open. Note that the address bar shows the folder's location on the computer—Local Disk (C:), in this case.

Still only two windows open
Address bar

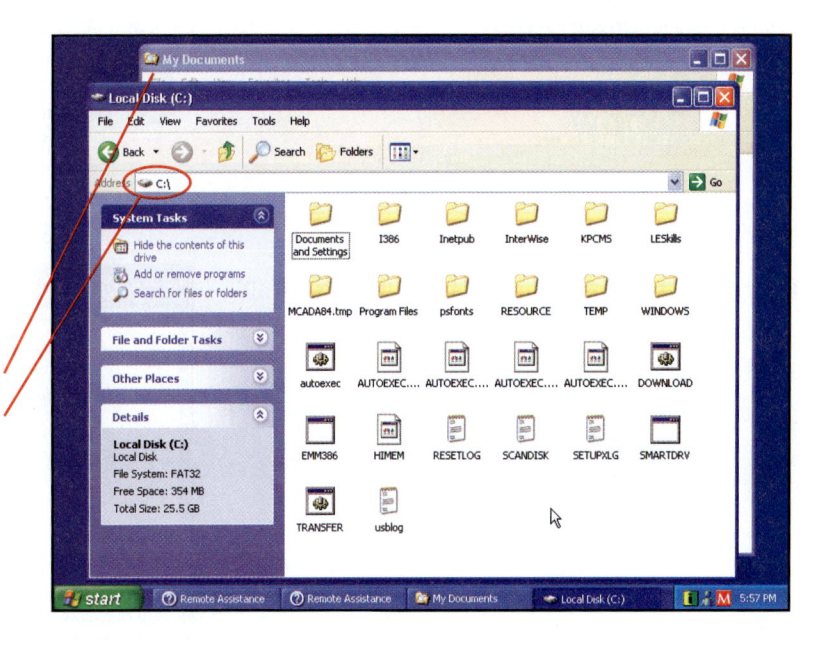

> **IN DEPTH**
>
> The Windows XP default configuration setting opens all folders in the same window. What is being demonstrated here is another option for ending up with the same result. Changing the default setting and using this technique allows you to choose when you want the folders to open in the same window. If your computer is configured to open folders in the same window, holding the Ctrl key down when double-clicking (or opening) additional folders opens them in separate windows. In other words, for folder navigation the Ctrl key lets you choose when to apply the opposite of what you have set in your configuration options.

Task 3   Switching to the Windows Explorer View   WIN   47

5 Hold the Ctrl key down and double-click the **Documents and Settings** folder.

This opens the Documents and Settings folder in the same window.

Hold the Ctrl key down and double-click the folder inside the Documents and Settings folder that has your user name (Rich, in this example).

This opens the user folder in the same window.

Hold the Ctrl key down and double-click the **My Documents** folder.

This opens your My Documents folder in the same window. You should now still only have two windows on your desktop, but notice that both are named the same. Clicking on the title bar of one window and then the next shows you that the two windows, although named the same, are actually different views of the same folder. Clicking on the Folders button of each shows you that you have arrived at the same location using two separate navigation techniques.

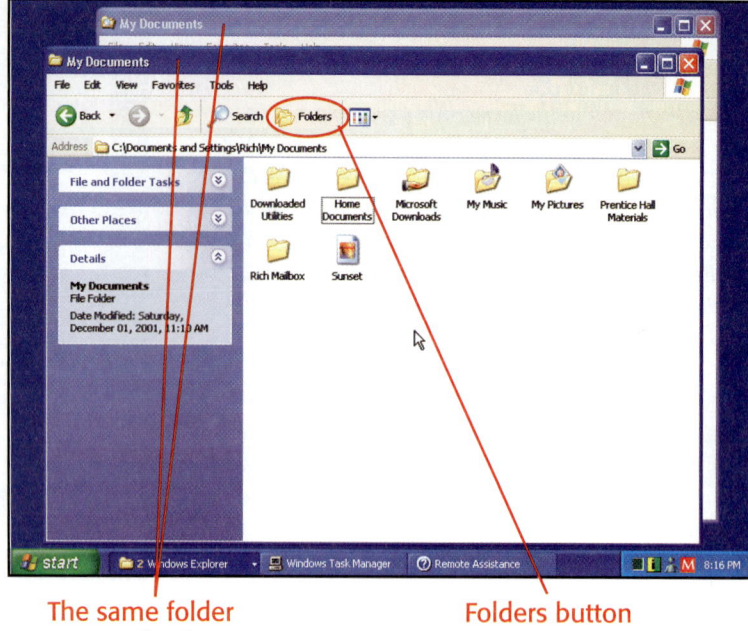

The same folder opened twice

Folders button

QUICK TIP

If you want to see both folders at the same time equally sharing the available desktop space, right-click on an empty space in the taskbar, slide to and click on either the Tile Windows Horizontally or Tile Windows Vertically option.

6 Click the **Close** button on the title bars of all open windows.

This puts you back on the empty desktop.

Click the **Start** button, right-click the **My Documents** icon, and then slide to and click the **Explore** option.

This displays the Windows Explorer view of the My Documents window. Notice that the Folders button is already pressed in the toolbar, and the My Documents folder is highlighted and opened (expanded) in the left pane. The contents of the My Documents folder are displayed in the right pane.

Left pane already expanded and My Documents highlighted
My Computer not expanded

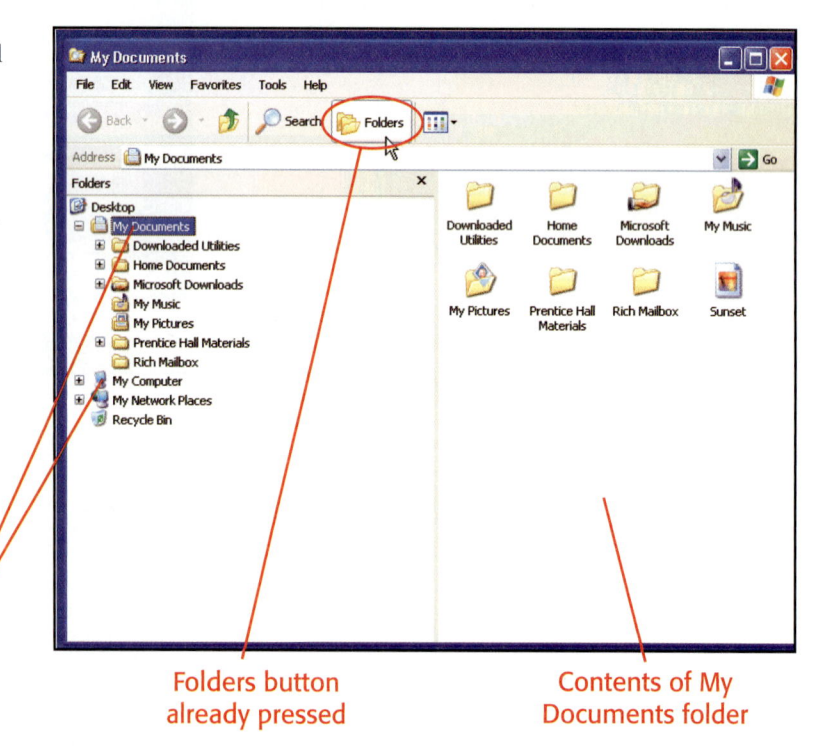

Folders button already pressed

Contents of My Documents folder

48 WIN Lesson 2 Working with Folders and Files

7 In the left pane, highlight **My Computer** by clicking once on the name itself.

This displays the contents of My Computer in the right pane. Notice that the plus (+) sign is no longer displayed. It has changed to a minus (−) sign and the folder's contents are displayed below the name. This is called **expanding** *the folder. Notice that the My Documents folder no longer shows its contents and that the − sign has changed to a + sign. This is called* **collapsing** *the folder. When you pass your mouse pointer over the folder's name, you should see it change to a hyperlink. To expand a folder and collapse all other folders in addition to displaying the folder's contents on the right, make sure you click the hyperlinked words to the right of the icon and not the + sign. Simply clicking the + sign opens the folders but does not display the contents.*

My Documents folder collapses
Click name to expand
Pointer changes name to hyperlink

8 In the left pane, click the plus (+) sign beside **My Documents** to expand the My Documents folder.

Notice that this does not display the contents of My Documents in the right pane even though the + sign is no longer displayed. The right pane still displays the contents of My Computer, which remains expanded.

Click the **My Pictures** folder.

Passing your mouse pointer over the name turns it into a hyperlink, but clicking on it only highlights the folder rather than opening it. This is because there are only files (or shortcuts) stored in the folder. If additional folders were in there, a + sign would have been displayed to the left of its icon.

My Computer still expanded
Files in My Pictures folder
Shortcut to Sample Pictures folder in My Pictures folder

My Documents folder expanded
My Pictures folder highlighted

IN DEPTH

The Sample Pictures folder displayed in the right pane of the My Pictures folder is a shortcut. You can identify a shortcut by the small upward-curving arrow in its lower-left corner. You can use shortcuts as a quick way to access an object from different locations on the computer. The Sample Pictures folder is actually stored in another folder but it appears as if it is stored in the My Pictures folder. Double-clicking on that shortcut activates the real Sample Pictures folder just as though it were double-clicked. Shortcuts allow you to put a virtual copy of an object at numerous locations, but you only have to update the one original when you need to make changes.

Notice, too, that the shortcut folder displays miniature versions of the image files stored within the actual folder. This is an example of the level of graphics Microsoft uses in Windows XP.

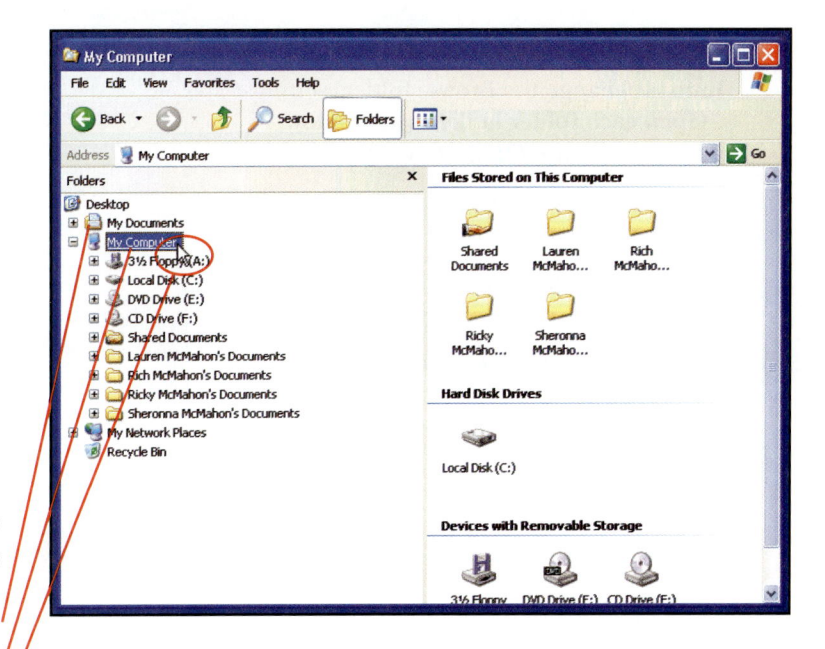

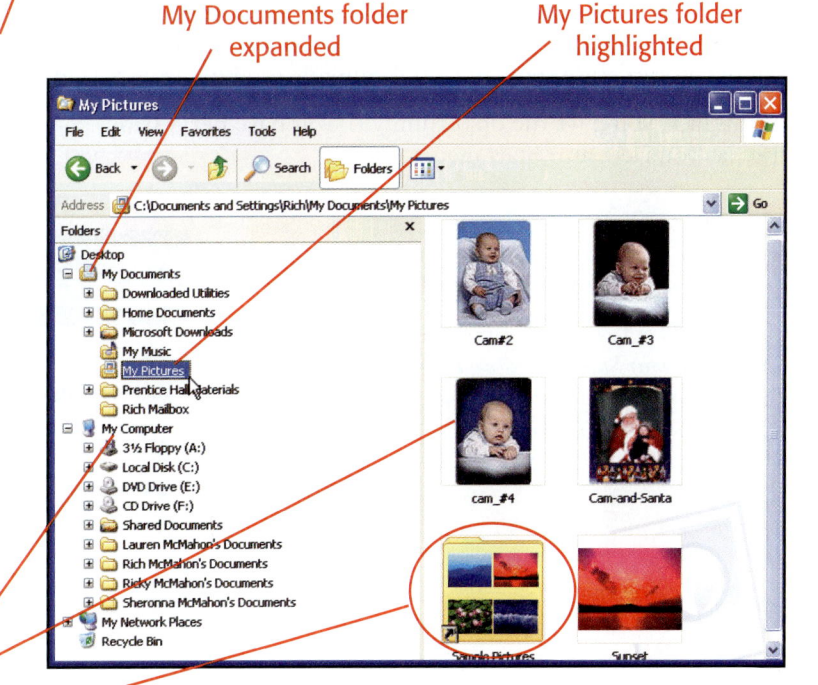

Task 3 Switching to the Windows Explorer View   WIN   49

9 Click the **Tools** menu and select **Folder Options**. Change the Browse folders setting to **Open each folder in the same window**, and then click the **OK** button.

This changes back to the default folder browsing configuration, with each folder opening in the same window.

Click the **Close** button on the My Pictures window.

This closes the My Pictures window and brings you back to your clean desktop.

Task 4
CUSTOMIZING THE START MENU

Why would I do this?
One of the main attractions of Windows XP is that it provides you with the ability to customize your environment. Here is another example of how you can do just that in a location that you will use frequently. You also have the chance to see where you can erase some of your frequently used items displayed by Windows XP.

In this task, you have the opportunity (if you have permission) to make changes to the way you view your Start menu.

1 Click the **Start** button. Right-click the blank, blue space next to the **Log Off** and **Turn Off Computer** buttons.

This opens your Start menu, and then opens its Properties option in the shortcut menu (even though it has only one option in that menu).

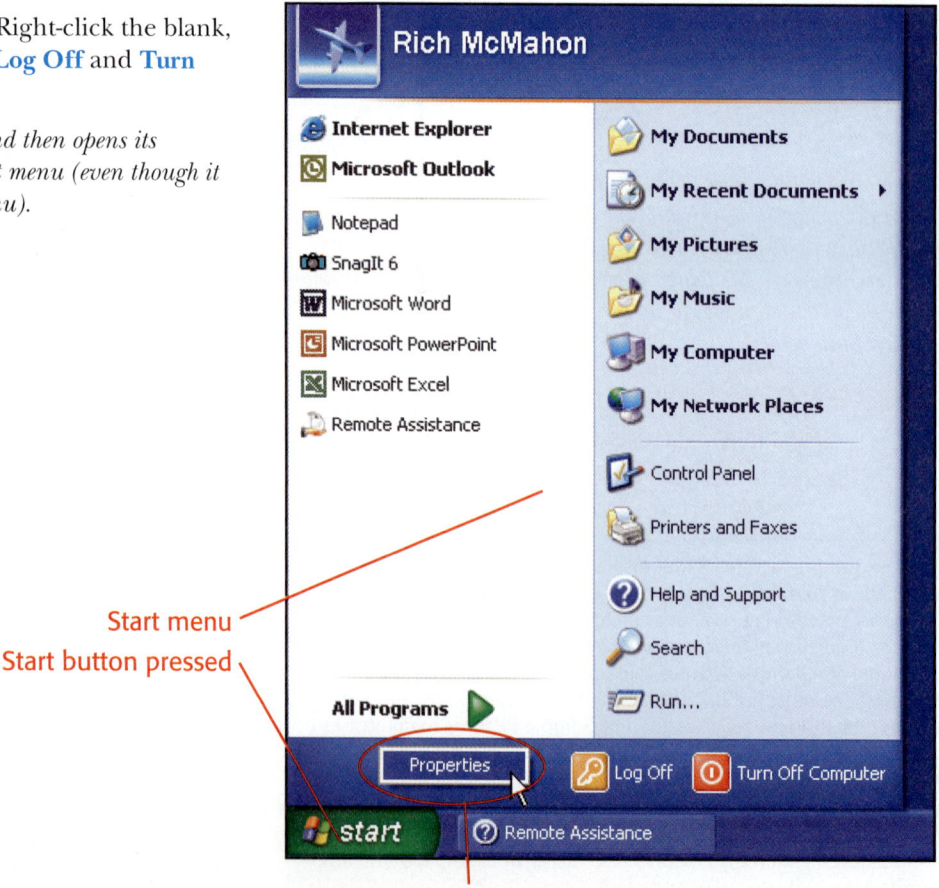

Start menu
Start button pressed
Properties option highlighted

50   WIN   Lesson 2   Working with Folders and Files

② Click the **Properties** option.

This opens the Taskbar and Start Menu Properties dialog box.

Click the **Start Menu** tab.

This allows you to make changes to the view your system displays when you click the Start button and open its Start menu. Notice that there are two choices, and each one has a Customize button where you can make additional changes to the Start menu's configuration.

Start menu tab
Menu style option buttons
Customize buttons
OK, Cancel, and Apply buttons

> **CAUTION**
> The default for this Start menu setting has the Start menu option button selected. Your computer's setup may be different if your administrator changed this for some reason. If so, complete the items in the next step but you should return to the original configuration prior to completing this task.

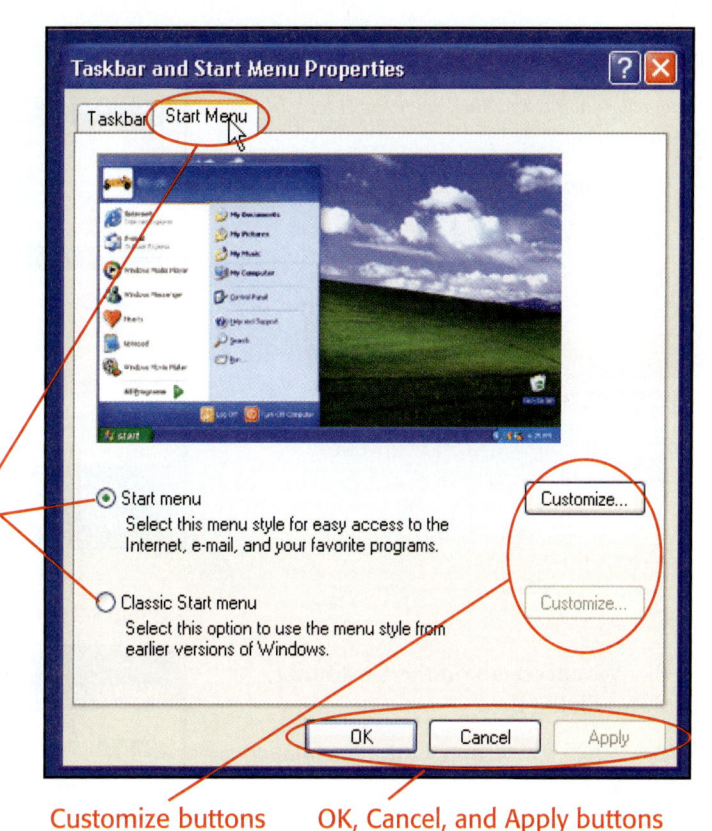

③ Click the **Classic Start menu** option button.

The preview inside the dialog box shows you what a sample desktop will look like if you click Apply or OK to choose the Classic Start menu option.

Style demonstrated
Classic Start menu option

Task 4 Customizing the Start Menu WIN 51

4 Click the **Start menu** option button.

You see a preview of what the Start menu will look like if you select this option.

Click the **Customize** button.

The Customize Start Menu dialog box displays.

Customize Start menu dialog box
Start menu option
Number of programs on Start menu setting

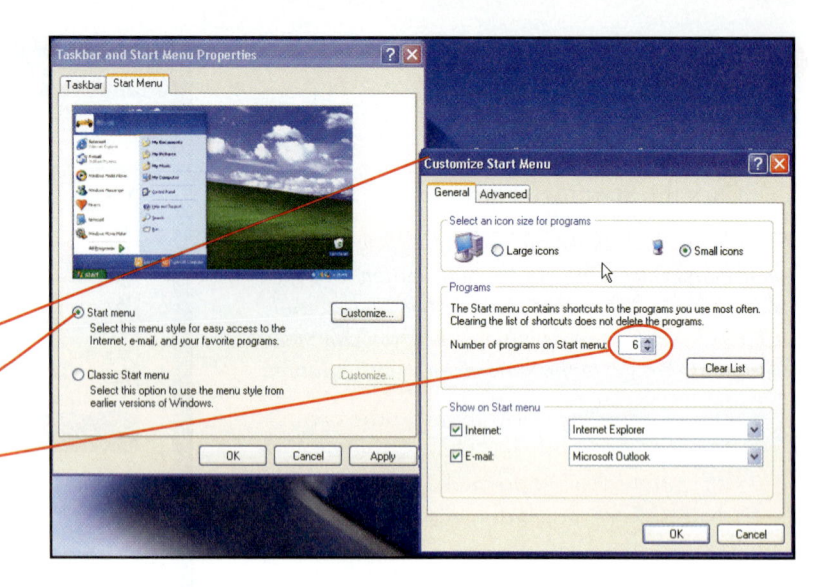

5 Click the **Advanced** tab on the Customize Start Menu dialog box.

This provides access to the advanced settings available for customizing the Start menu.

Use the scroll bar in the Start menu items list to scroll down so that the option buttons for My Computer are displayed.

Using the scroll bar lets you access any of the option buttons available.

Click the **Display as a menu** selection, and then click the **Clear List** button.

The Display as a menu option lets you choose the items in submenus rather than clicking on links for direct access. The Clear List button in the Recent Documents section of the dialog box erases the listing in the Start menu that shows your most recently opened documents. Notice the statement informing you that erasing the list does not delete the documents themselves.

Advanced tab
My Computer options
Display as a menu option
Scroll bar
Clear List button

52 WIN Lesson 2 Working with Folders and Files

6 If you have permission to change your computer's settings, click **OK** in the Customize Start Menu dialog box, and then click **OK** in the Taskbar and Start Menu Properties dialog box to return to the desktop. Otherwise, click the **Cancel** button in both dialog boxes to arrive back at the desktop.

This either implements or cancels the configuration settings you made. In either case, you end up back at the clean desktop.

If you have permission to make the change, click the **Start** button and click the **My Computer** icon. Then click the **Start** button again to close the menu.

This lets you verify the changes you made in your configuration by noting the right arrow that is available along with a pull-out listing for the My Computer items.

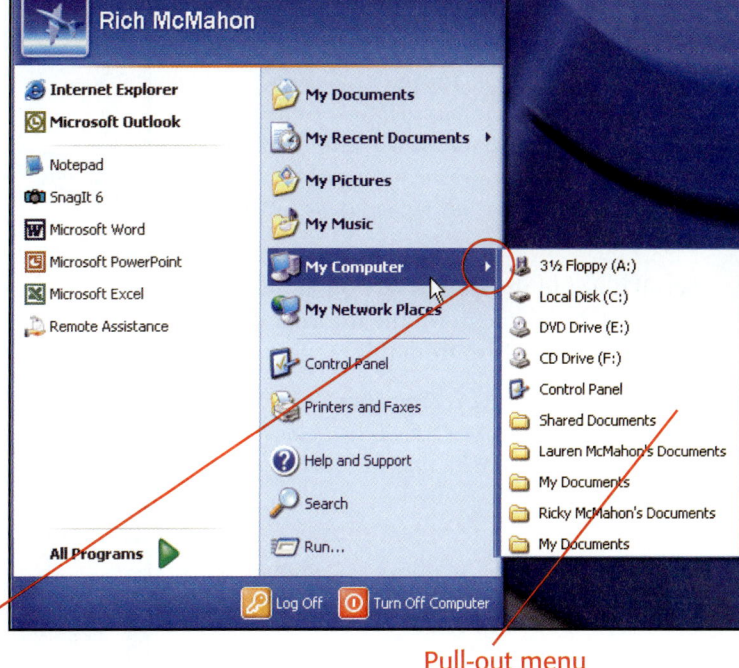

Right arrow

Pull-out menu

QUICK TIP
You can still open the My Computer folder itself and ignore the pull-out menu by right-clicking on the Start menu's My Computer option and then clicking on the Open or the Explore option.

Task 5
GATHERING HARD DRIVE DETAILS

Why would I do this?
Often you need information about a particular object. In this case, we show you how to determine the space availability on your hard drive for additional storage.

In this task, you use My Computer to help you verify the details about your hard drive's capacity.

1 Click the **Start** button. Right-click on **My Computer** and click the **Open** option.

This opens your Start menu and then opens your My Computer folder using the shortcut menu.

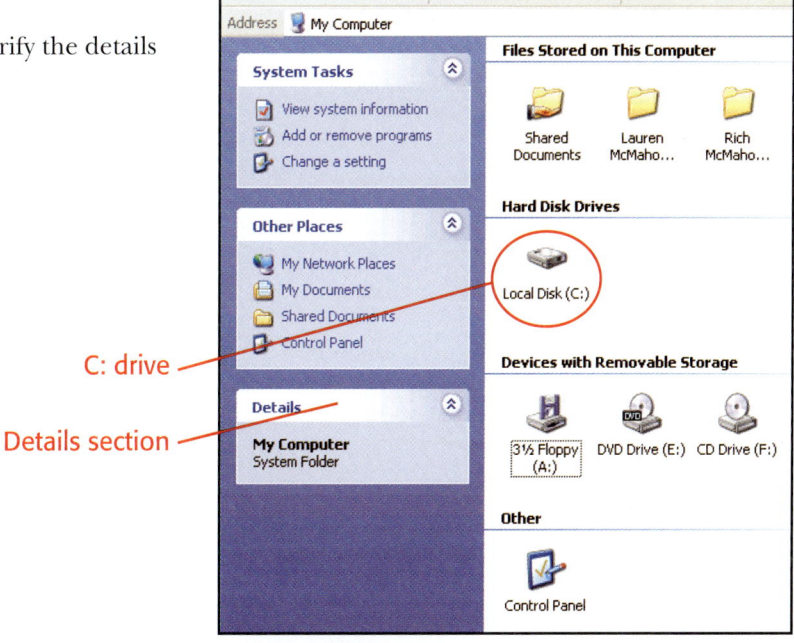

C: drive

Details section

Task 5   Gathering Hard Drive Details   WIN   53

2 Double-click the hard disk drive icon (**C:**, in this example).

This opens the C: folder and displays its contents. Notice that the left pane has four context-sensitive areas displayed (you may need to use the scroll bar to see all of them). The information you are seeking about your hard disk drive is in the Details section at the bottom section of the left pane.

Scroll down to the **Details** section, if necessary, and then write down the information about your disk drive from this section.

*In this example, the C: drive is configured as a FAT 32 file system, with a capacity of 25.5 GB (**gigabytes**; one gigabyte equals 1024 MB), and 375 MB of remaining free space.*

Context-sensitive areas
Details area
Detail information

> **QUICK TIP**
> If the bottom section of the left pane is not visible, click the double-down arrows to reveal the contents. In the sample used for this exercise, half of the arrows in the four sections face upward. Those other sections are closed and the arrows point downward instead.

3 Click the **Close** button on the Local Disk and My Computer windows.

This closes the windows and puts you back at your desktop.

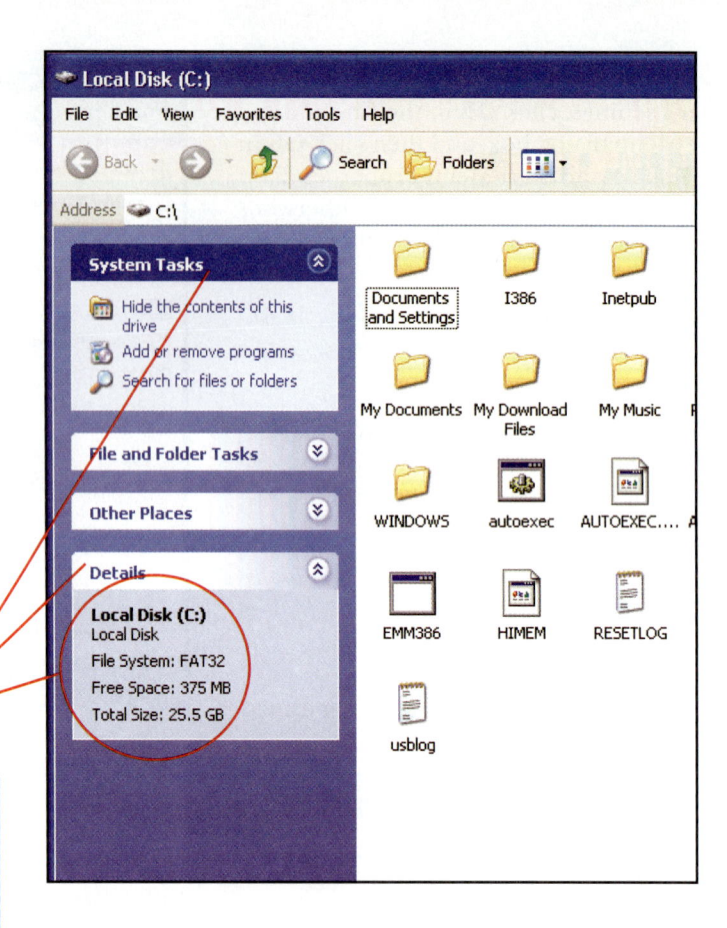

Task 6
USING THE SEARCH FEATURE

Why would I do this?

Finding something you stored a long time ago often turns into a difficult task. This can become even more challenging if you are working with objects on your computer. You will likely welcome any assistance available to you that can ease the burden. The Windows XP search feature, which offers such assistance, is always available. Knowing how to use it correctly can often save you significant time.

In this task, you use the search feature to locate a file you stored on your computer.

1 Click the **Start** button, and slide up to and click the **Search** icon (with the magnifying glass) on the right side of the Start menu.

This opens the Search Results window.

What do you want to search for
All files and folders

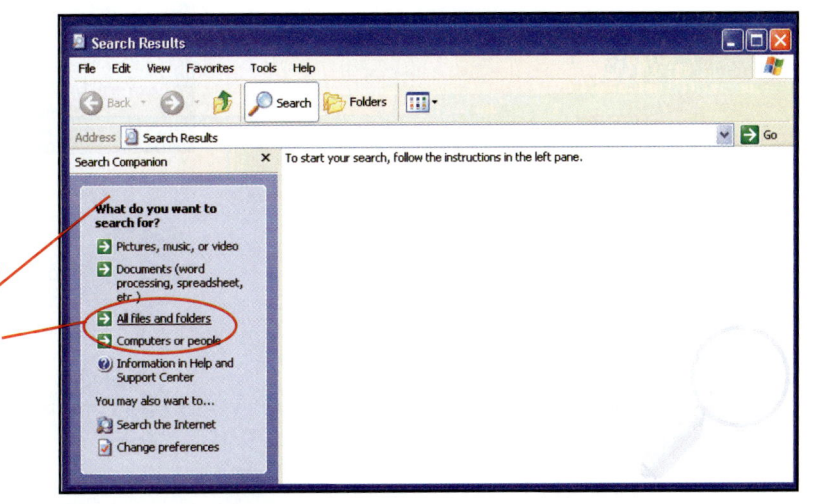

2 Answer the question, "What do you want to search for?" at the top of the left pane by clicking on the **All files and folders** selection.

This opens the left pane into another section that allows you to furnish search criteria.

Search criteria
Default search location
Search button

IN DEPTH

By default, Windows XP searches for the requested objects on the local hard drives but it can be directed to search another location by choosing another selection in the Look in drop-down list.

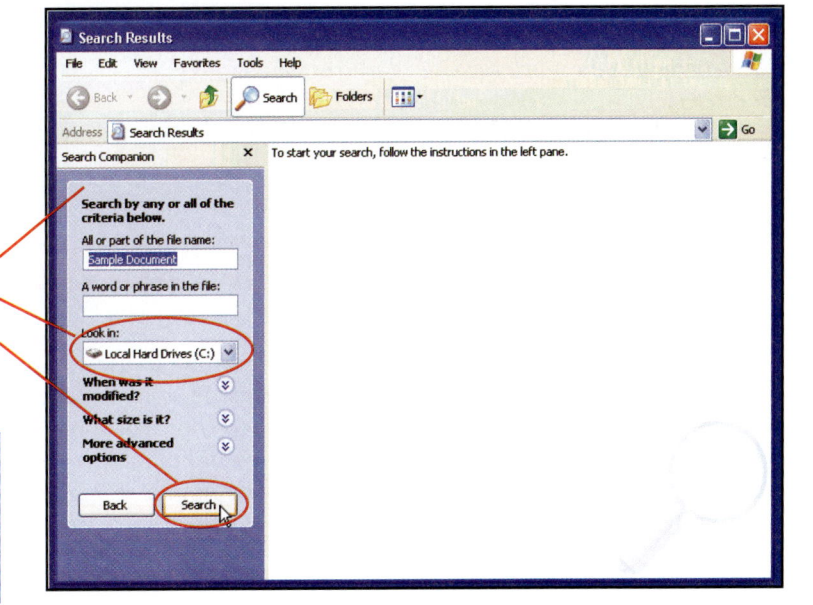

Task 6   Using the Search Feature   WIN   55

3 Search your computer to locate the document that you created in Lesson 1 by entering its name, **Sample Document**, in the **All or part of the file name** text box, and clicking the Search button to initiate your search.

After a brief delay, the search results are returned. If your file has been deleted and removed from your computer, the results will not include your file. You can perform operations (such as open, copy, move, or even delete) on any of the objects found in the search.

Search results
Instances of found object
Different objects with same name

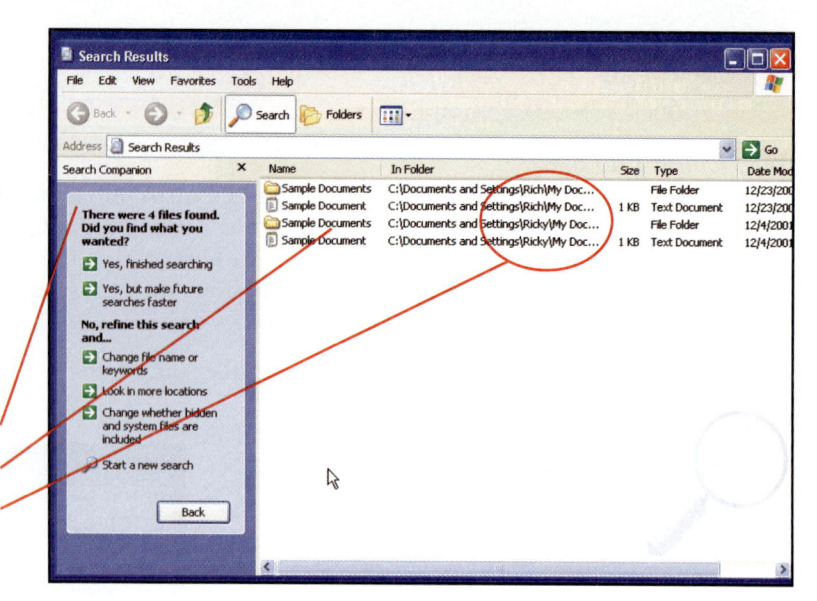

IN DEPTH You may see other items listed in your search results as well. For example, notice that the example shows another file named Sample Document, located in a different folder, in addition to two folders with the same name. They are different because one set is located in Rich's Documents and Settings folder and the other is located in Ricky's Documents and Settings folder.

4 Click the Search Results window's Close button.

This terminates your search request and returns you to the desktop.

Task 7
FORMATTING A FLOPPY DISK

Why would I do this?
You will do much of your practice work (while learning to use computers) on multiple workstations. Normally you will not have storage rights on those computers. Additionally, it will be in your best interest to keep copies of your work. *Floppy disks* provide you with a convenient storage medium that is easy to use and widely available. *Formatting* is the action taken on a computer storage medium (such as a floppy disk) in order for you to store your data for future use.

In this task, you learn to format a floppy disk.

❶ If you do not need a floppy disk, skip this task. Otherwise, obtain a non-write-protected, blank High Density (HD) floppy disk. Insert the floppy disk into your computer's *floppy disk drive*, the mechanism used to read or write information to or from a floppy disk.

Ensure that the disk is not write-protected by flipping it over and verifying that the slider hole in the corner of the disk is in the closed position. If that slider is open, your disk is write-protected and you will not be able to format it; slide it to the closed position.

With your floppy disk inserted, click the **Start** button, and then slide up to and click the **My Computer** option.

This opens your My Computer folder.

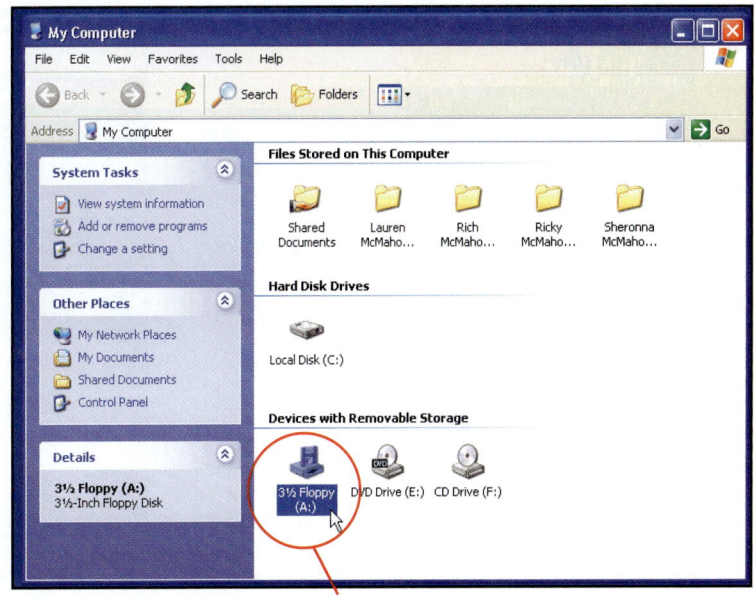

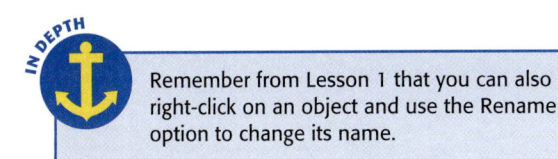

A – 3½ Floppy (A:) icon

❷ Right-click the **3½ Floppy (A:)** icon, and click the **Format** option in the shortcut menu.

This opens the Format 3½ Floppy (A:) dialog box.

In the **Volume label** box, type the following name for your floppy disk: **SAMPLE**.

This enters the typed name as the volume label (or disk's name).

Remember from Lesson 1 that you can also right-click on an object and use the Rename option to change its name.

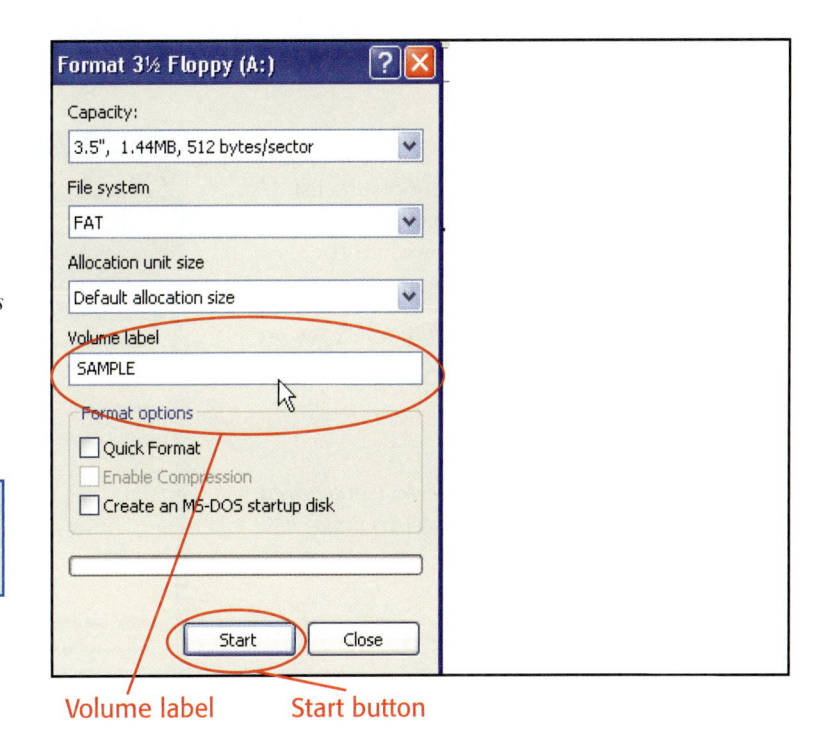

Volume label   Start button

Task 7   Formatting a Floppy Disk   WIN   **57**

3 Press and hold down the ⊞ key and then press the F1 key.

This opens the Help and Support Center window.

In the **Search** box, type **Quick Format** and click the green arrow.

This begins a search for information on Quick Format.

Quick Format in Search box
Click to start search

> **QUICK TIP**
> To get to the Help and Support Center, you can also go through the Start menu by clicking (and releasing) ⊞ and then pressing H. Additionally, to obtain some information about Quick Format, you can simply right-click the words Quick Format in the Format 3½" Floppy (A:) dialog box, and choose What's This in the shortcut menu. A pop-up description gives you part of the same warning revealed in this exercise.

4 In the Search Results pane on the left, click the **Format a disk** item in the results list. Use the scroll bar in the right pane of the Help and Support Center window when the Search Results window appears.

This reveals the portion of the search in which you are interested. Note the information regarding when you should use the Quick Format option.

Click the **Close** button.

This closes the Help and Support Center window and returns you to the Format 3½" Floppy (A:) dialog box.

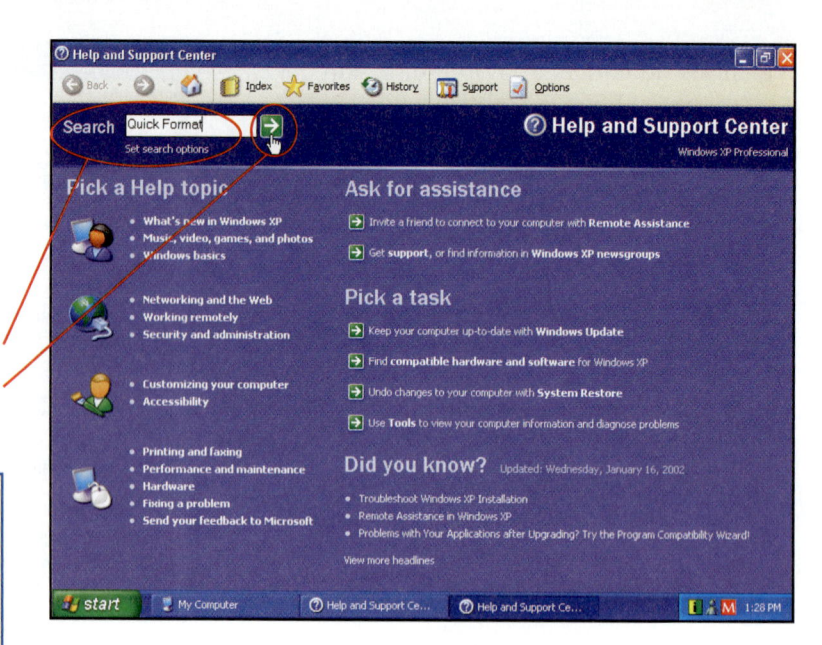

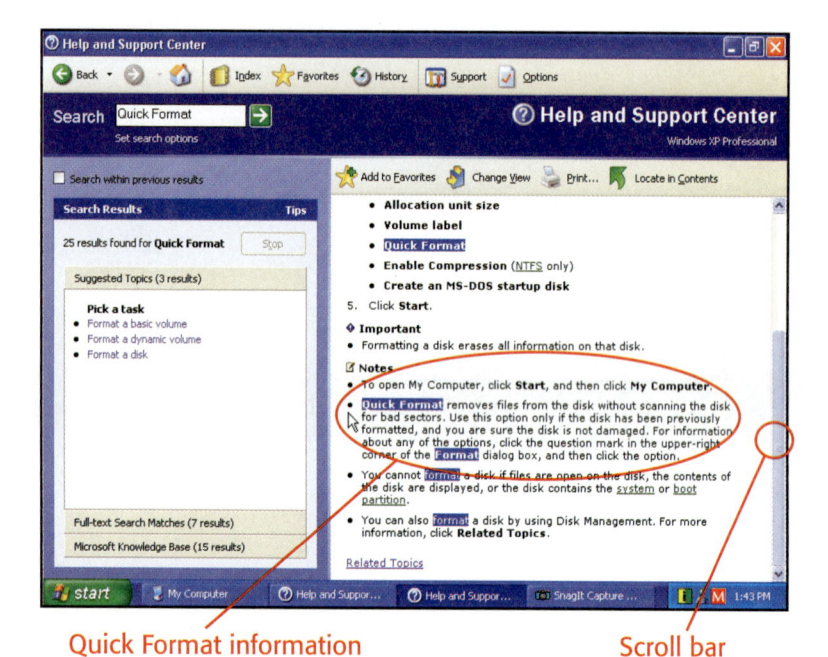

Quick Format information   Scroll bar

> **CAUTION**
> Unless you are instructed to use them, or you are familiar with the possible outcomes from their use, the first three options at the top of the Format 3½" Floppy (A:) dialog box (Capacity, File system, and Allocation unit size) should be left alone.

5 In the **Format options** section, ensure that the boxes are all unchecked and click the **Start** button to initiate your format action. Click the **OK** button to confirm the warning.

Once you confirm the warning about erasing all the data on the disk, your disk formatting begins.

Observe the disk format progress in the white box at the bottom of the dialog box.

When the formatting begins, the green progress indicator starts filling the white box to represent the disk formatting progress. Note that when the formatting is complete a Format Complete dialog box appears.

Close button
Format Complete dialog box

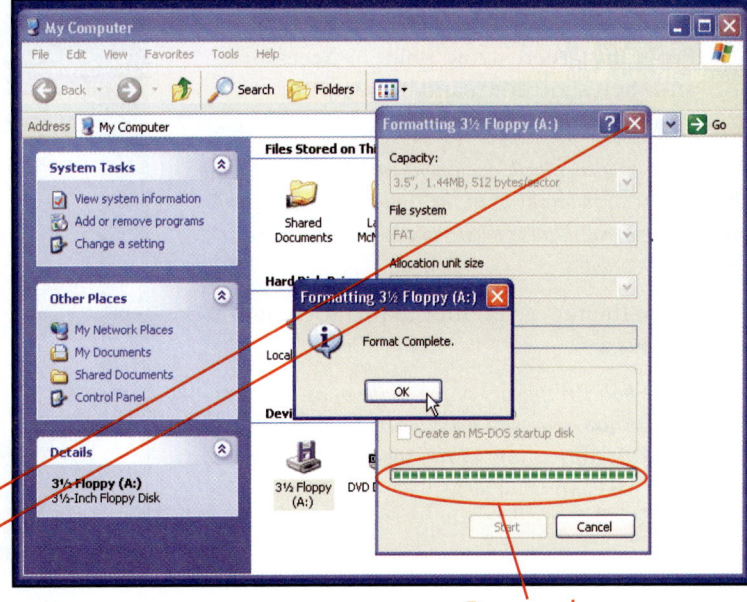

Progress box

QUICK TIP
For faster disk formatting, check the Quick Format option in the Format options section.

6 When your disk formatting is complete, click the **OK** button.

This closes the Format Complete dialog box.

Since you are not formatting any additional floppies, click the **Close** button (either the one at the bottom or the top right) to return to the My Computer window. Then close the My Computer window.

This brings you back to the desktop.

Task 8
OPENING AND CLOSING AN APPLICATION

Why would I do this?
Much of your work involves choosing an application that is loaded on your computer and then creating files with those applications. One such application, WordPad, is included with Windows XP. You will use it to create and print a new file.

In this task, you learn how to open, use, print from, and then close an application found on your Start menu.

Task 8   Opening and Closing an Application   WIN   59

❶ Click the **Start** button, click the **All Programs** green arrow, point to **Accessories**, and then slide down and click on the **WordPad** option.

This opens a new, blank document in WordPad. Notice that the cursor is blinking in the upper-left corner of the large white area. This is where you begin entering text into the document.

Move the mouse pointer to the document's text area.

The mouse pointer appears in the shape of an I-beam that you can use, once you have text entered into the document, to position your cursor wherever you want to make your next entry.

Blinking cursor
I-beam pointer
Document window can be resized as necessary

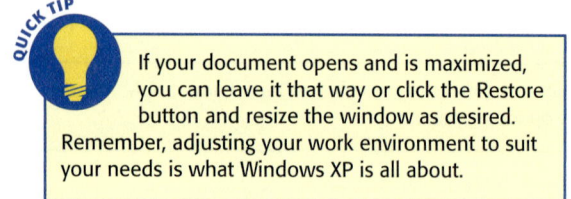

> **QUICK TIP**
> If your document opens and is maximized, you can leave it that way or click the Restore button and resize the window as desired. Remember, adjusting your work environment to suit your needs is what Windows XP is all about.

❷ Click either a blank space on the taskbar or a blank space on your desktop, and then click on a blank space in the WordPad document's text area.

This makes the text document an inactive window (and your blinking cursor disappears) and then activates it again (and brings the cursor back into view).

Click the **Date/Time** button on the toolbar, click the **OK** button to accept the selected date format, and then press ⏎Enter to move the cursor to the next line. Then type your name on one line, type **Windows XP's WordPad Assignment** on the next line, type the name of your company on the next line, and then press ⏎Enter.

This enters the designated text into the upper-left corner of the document's text area with your cursor below your last line of text. Notice that your text is entered where your cursor is and not where the I-beam is located.

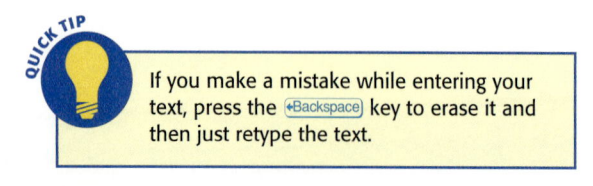

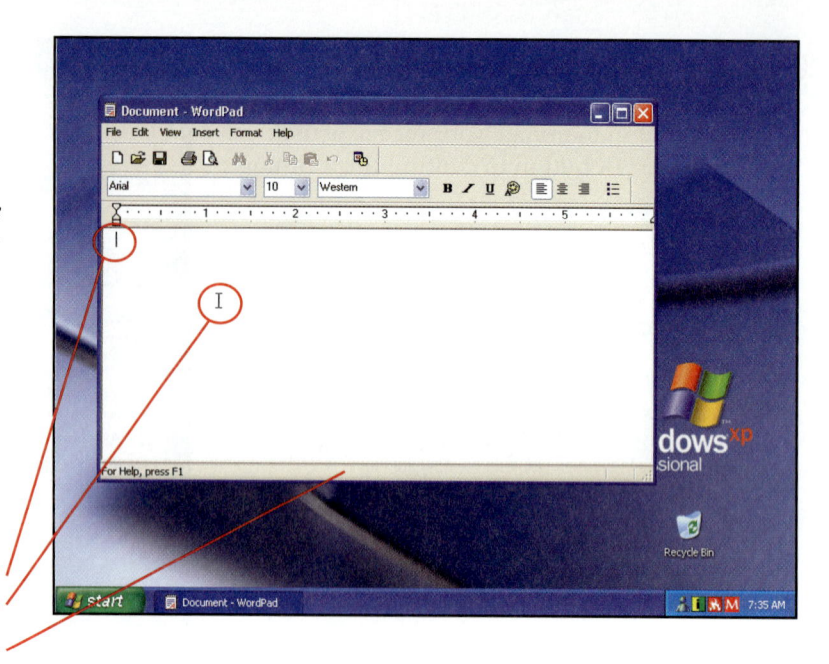

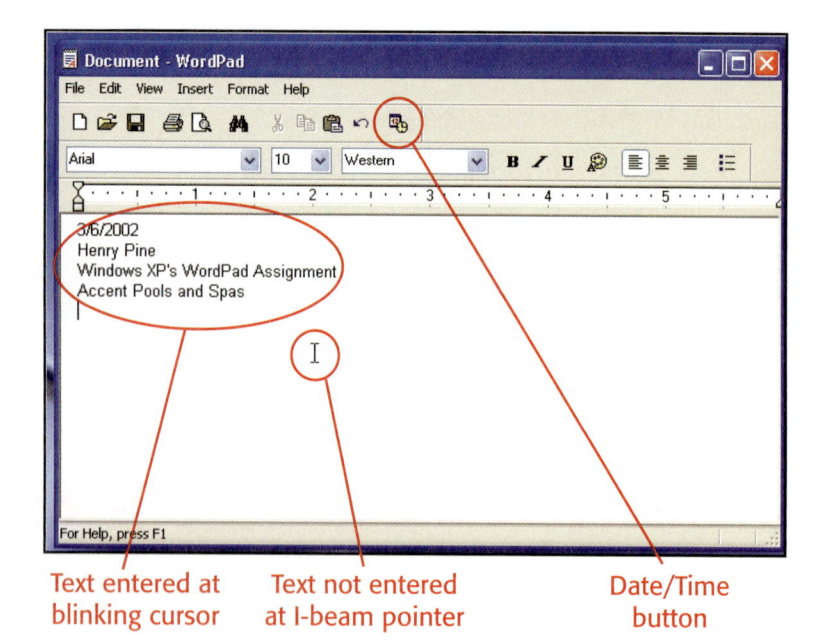

Text entered at blinking cursor
Text not entered at I-beam pointer
Date/Time button

> **QUICK TIP**
> If you make a mistake while entering your text, press the ⌫Backspace key to erase it and then just retype the text.

60 WIN Lesson 2 Working with Folders and Files

3 Triple-click the word **Windows** in the third line.

This highlights the entire line of text.

Drag the highlighted text to the space below your company's name.

As you drag the text, you see a vertical bar that indicates where the text will appear when you release the mouse button. The assignment information now appears below the company name.

Triple-click the date in your top line of text, and drag the highlighted date to the line below the assignment information.

This relocates the highlighted information to the new location and automatically moves all the other items up in the block of text.

Date still highlighted after being triple-clicked and dragged

Reordered lines of text

Center button on Format bar

Format bar

4 Press the Ctrl+A key combination.

This highlights the entire block of text. Notice that it also highlights the blank line you added at the end of your text.

Click the **Center** button on the Format bar.

The buttons on WordPad's Format bar enable you to change the size, color, position, and effects of the characters you use in your document. Clicking the Center button while the text is highlighted centers the entire block on your page.

Click the **Maximize** button.

This fills your screen so you can see the entire effect of your actions.

Ruler

Centered text block includes trailing empty blank line

Centered block of text (text may appear "off-center" to the right)

CAUTION

After you click the Center button, the document may not appear to be centered within the margins (as shown in the figure). However, the text is properly centered when you preview or print the document.

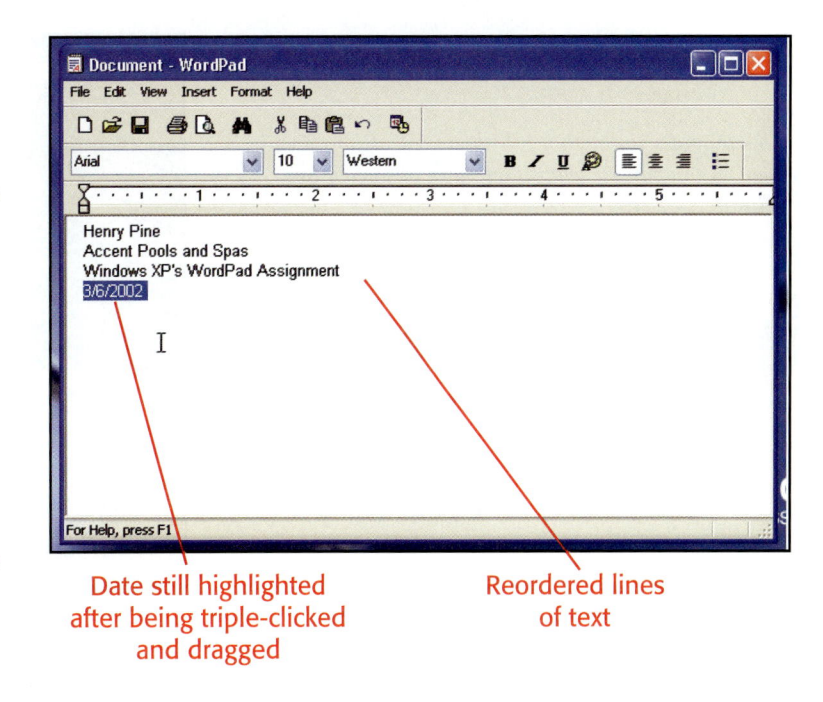

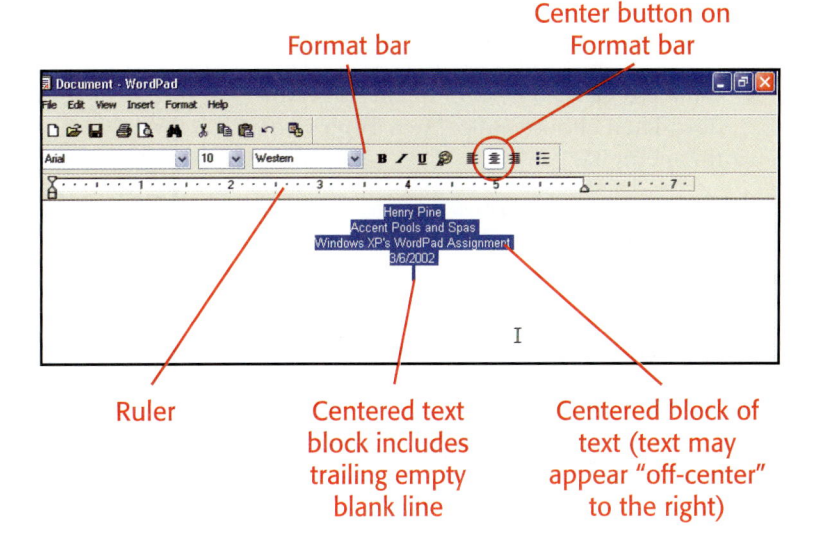

Task 8 Opening and Closing an Application WIN 61

5 Click the **Print Preview** button in the toolbar.

This provides you with a full-sheet view of your document so you can see what it will look like when you print it.

Click the **Zoom In** button at the top of your preview window.

This zooms in the view of your page and lets you increase the size of what you see. Notice the Print button that you could click if your document were finished and you wanted to send it to the printer.

Print button
Zoom In button
Close button

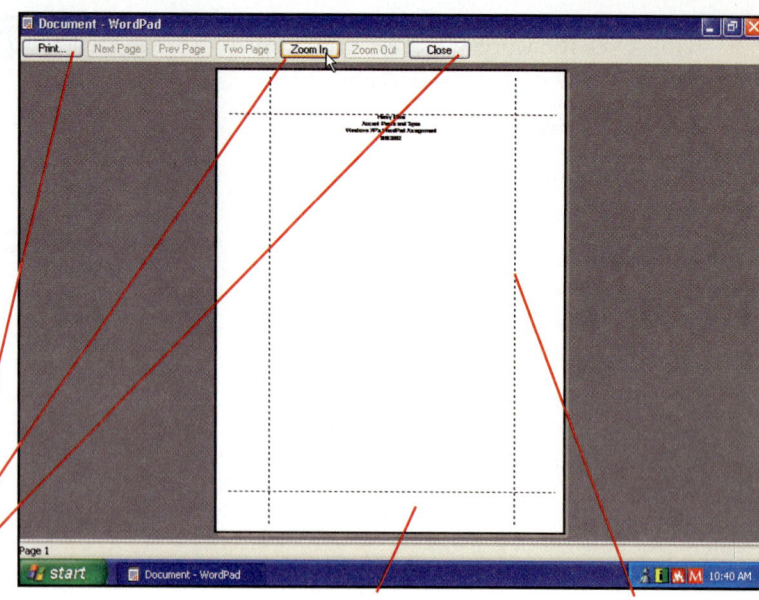

Full-sheet view of your document
Margin indicators

Help window's overview of WordPad
Overview's first 10 words

6 Click the **Close** button in the preview window. Then choose **Help**, **Help Topics** from the menu bar.

This returns you to the document window, and opens WordPad Help and displays an information page that gives you an overview of WordPad.

Right click a blank space on your taskbar, and then select **Tile Windows Horizontally**.

With two windows open, this fits both the Help window and your text document window into your available desktop space.

Type the first 10 words of the overview's initial paragraph into the last empty line of your text document.

This adds the information from the overview to your document.

WordPad's Help menu
Horizontally tiled document shown as active in taskbar
Typed copy of first 10 words

QUICK TIP

If your horizontal-tiling action incorporates more than just the intended two windows shown in the example, simply close any unwanted windows and reapply the tiling action through the taskbar once again.

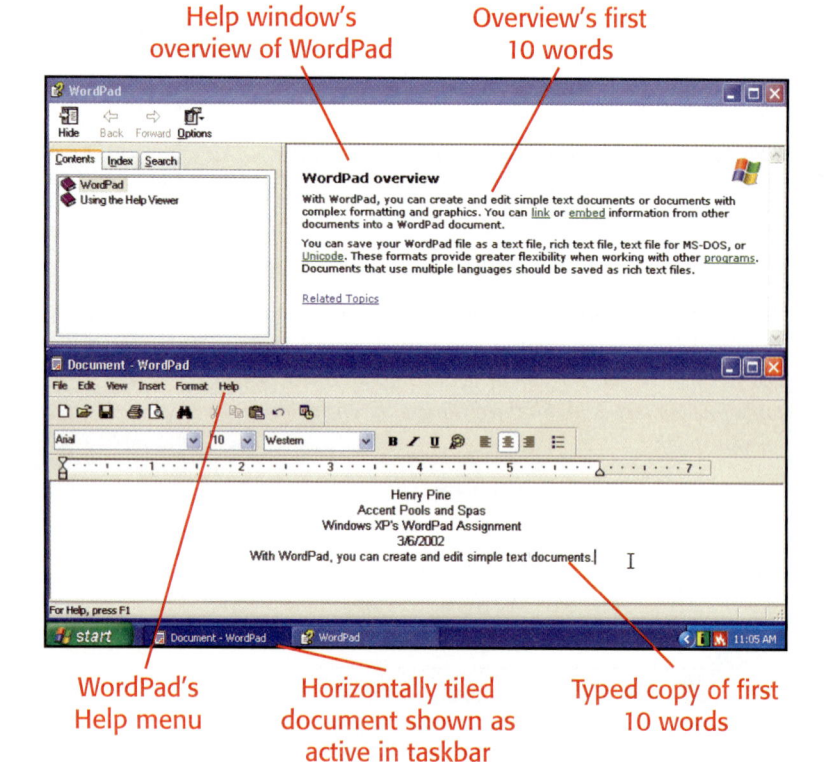

WIN Lesson 2 Working with Folders and Files

7 Click the WordPad Help window's **Close** button, and then click the document's taskbar button. Choose **File**, **Print** and then click the **Print** button.

This opens the Print dialog box and sends your output to the default printer using its existing settings.

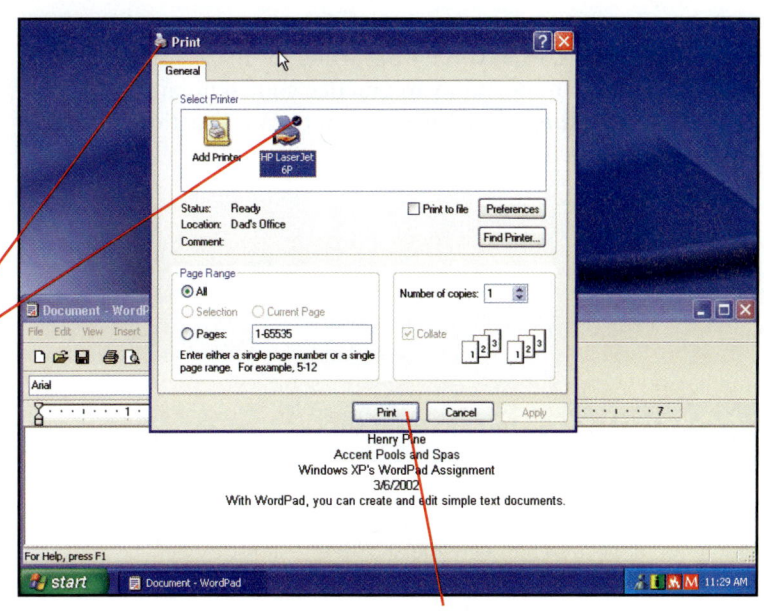

Print dialog box
Default printer

Print button

QUICK TIP

In many applications, you also can press Ctrl+P to display the Print dialog box. If you click the Print button on the toolbar, one copy of the document is immediately sent to the printer.

My Documents folder as default saving location

8 Choose **File**, **Save**. While the file name is still highlighted, type your two initials, the number **02**, and the word **assignment**, and then click the **Save** button.

This opens the Save As dialog box where you can change the highlighted file name and save the document (create a stored copy of the file) in your user's My Documents folder, if the default saving location has not been altered.

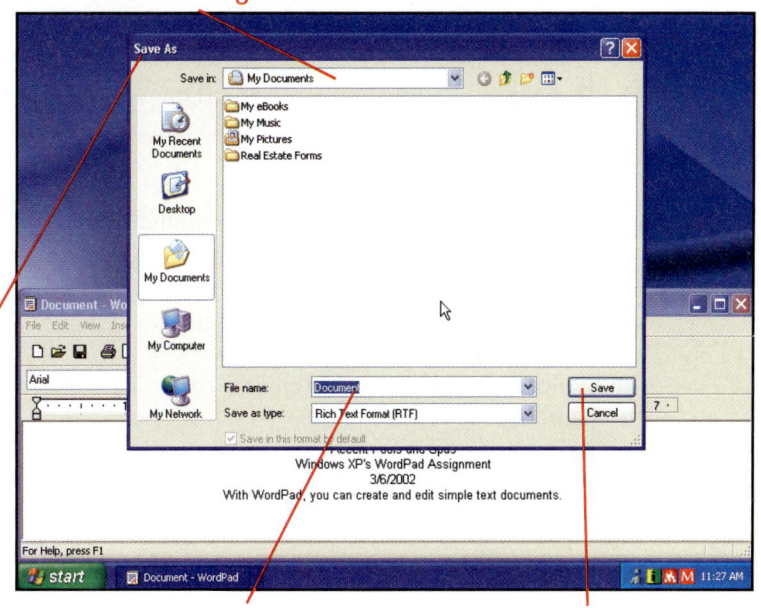

Save As dialog box

IN DEPTH

Notice that the Save As dialog box opens the first time you save a document. This forces you to enter a file name or decide to keep the default file name. When you subsequently save the same file by choosing **File**, **Save**, pressing Ctrl+S, or clicking the **Save** button on the toolbar, the Save As dialog box isn't displayed. The stored file is simply updated with any new information. If you want to keep your original saved file intact, you should choose the **File**, **Save As** command, and furnish a new file name in the Save As dialog box.

Document file name already highlighted for you to change

Save button

9 Click the **Close** button on your text document's window.

This closes the text document and returns you to the desktop.

Task 8   Opening and Closing an Application   WIN   **63**

The exercises that follow are designed for you to review and use what you have learned in this lesson. You also have the opportunity to practice your skills and then expand on them by applying them to new situations.

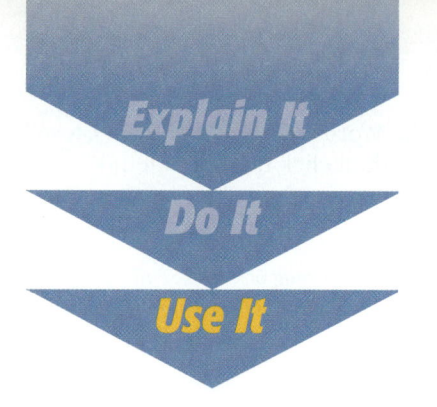

Explain It

Do It

Use It

COMPREHENSION

Comprehension exercises are designed to check your memory and understanding of the basic concepts in this lesson. You distinguish between true and false statements, identify new screen elements, and match terms with related statements. If you are uncertain of the correct answer, refer to the task number following each item (for example, T4 refers to Task 4) and review that task until you are confident that you can provide a correct response.

TRUE-FALSE

Circle either T or F.

T F 1. Clicking the middle button on the right end of the title bar always maximizes the window. **(T1)**

T F 2. Clicking the Folders button on the toolbar opens the selected folder. **(T3)**

T F 3. When you click the Folders button in the My Computer window, the Windows Explorer navigation pane replaces the action sidebar. **(T3)**

T F 4. By default, Windows XP opens each folder in its own window. **(T3)**

T F 5. The Start menu has a Properties option. **(T4)**

T F 6. After highlighting your C: drive's icon, you should click the double arrows so they face downward before you can read the details. **(T5)**

MATCHING QUESTIONS

A. Action sidebar   D. Search
B. Clear List   E. Ctrl
C. Control   F. Restore

Match the following statements to the word or phrase that is the best match from the list. Write the letter of the matching word or phrase in the space provided next to the number.

1. ____ Click on this half of the button's name to return the object's window to the size that it was before it was maximized. It is the middle one of the three buttons on the right side of the title bar. **(T1)**

2. ____ This menu is opened by pressing on the Alt key and then pressing Spacebar. **(T1)**

3. ____ This view replaces the Windows Explorer view in the left pane of an object's window. **(T3)**

4. ____ Hold this key down when double-clicking an object to open its window in an already opened window. **(T3)**

5. ____ Click this button to immediately remove your recently opened documents from your Start menu. **(T4)**

6. ____ Click on this Start Menu option to provides a means of querying the computer for its help locating a file you need. **(T6)**

64   WIN   Lesson 2   Working with Folders and Files

IDENTIFYING PARTS OF WINDOWS MANAGEMENT SCREENS

Refer to the figure and identify the numbered parts of the screen. Write the letter of the correct label in the space next to the number.

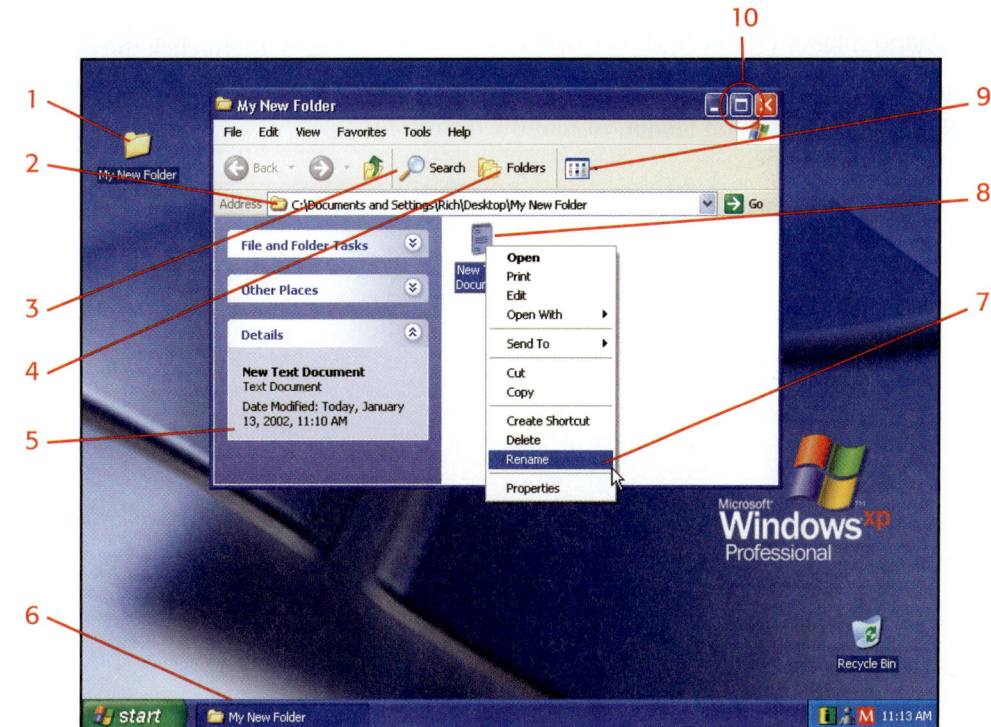

1. _____
2. _____
3. _____
4. _____
5. _____
6. _____
7. _____
8. _____
9. _____
10. _____

A. Use to switch navigating technique (T3)

B. Use to minimize the object (T1)

C. Use to fill the screen with object (T1)

D. A folder's icon (T1)

E. Use to help find files (T6)

F. Shows feature used to change the name of a file (T7)

G. Use to change how you view an object's contents (T1)

H. An object's full address is displayed here (T3)

I. Displays information on highlighted object (T5)

J. A document's icon (T1)

REINFORCEMENT

Reinforcement exercises are designed to reinforce the skills you learned by applying them to new situations. Detailed instructions are provided along with a figure, where appropriate, to illustrate the result. Complete the following reinforcement exercises sequentially.

R1—Copying a New Folder and Its Contents

1. Right-click on a blank area of your desktop, click on **New**, and then click on **Folder**. Accept the default name for the folder.
2. Double-click the **New Folder** icon to open it.
3. Right-click inside the New Folder window, click on **New**, and then click on **Text Document**. Accept the default file name.
4. Close the New Folder window.
5. Right-click on your **New Folder** icon, drag it to another blank area on your desktop, and then click on **Copy Here**.
6. Double-click the new **Copy of New Folder** icon, and notice that it also includes a copy of the New Text Document file that you created in the original folder. Close the folder.
7. Leave the folders on your desktop for the next exercise.

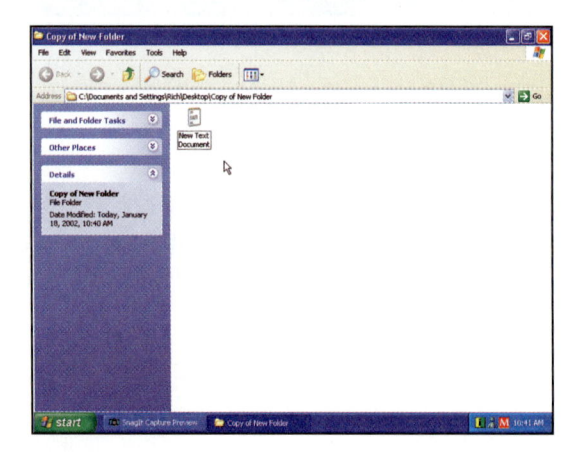

R2—Renaming Files

1. Locate the New Folder and Copy of New Folder folders and their contents from Reinforcement Exercise 1.
2. Open your Copy of New Folder folder, right-click the **New Text Document** file, and then click on **Rename**.
3. Type in the new name, **Test Text,** and press ⏎Enter.
4. Right-click the newly renamed **Test Text** document, drag it to a blank area in the Copy of New Folder window, and then click **Copy Here**. Notice that when copying, the original object remains intact.
5. Click on **Edit** in the menu bar, and click on **Select All**.
6. Right-click on one of the highlighted text documents and click on **Rename**.
7. Type **New Text Doc** and press ⏎Enter to rename both documents.
8. Close all open windows and leave the folders on your desktop for the next exercise.

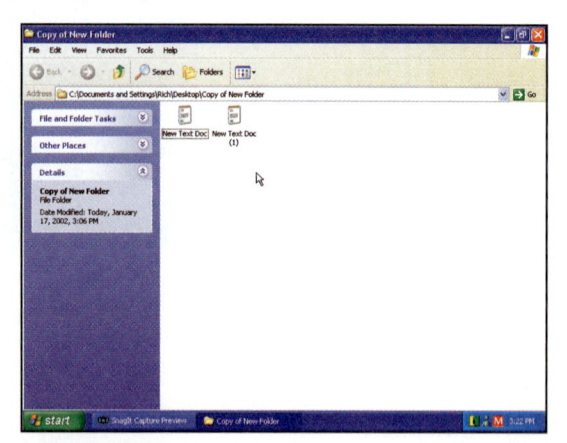

R3—Moving a Folder

1. Locate the New Folder and Copy of New Folder folders and their contents from Reinforcement Exercise 2.
2. Right-click the **Copy of New Folder** icon, drag it over to the New Folder icon, drop it on the **New Folder** icon, and then click on **Move Here**. Notice that in a Move operation, the original object does not remain intact. It moves to the new location.
3. Double-click the **New Folder** icon on your desktop. Verify that the moved object (Copy of New Folder) did actually move there.
4. Double-click the Copy of New Folder folder in the window, and verify that the contents also moved with the folder.

5. Close all open windows and leave the folder on your desktop for the next exercise.

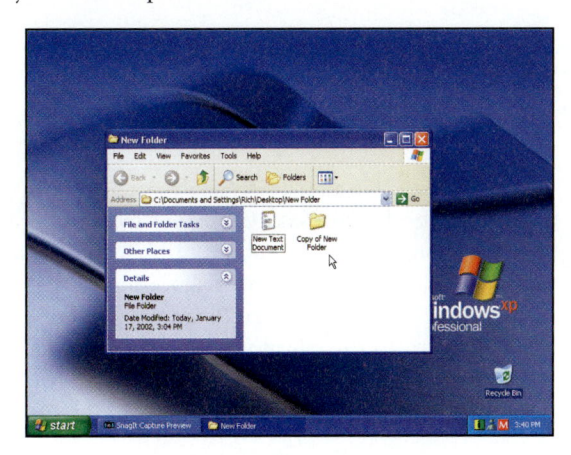

R4—Deleting and Restoring Files and Folders

1. Locate the New Folder icon with its Copy of New Folder folder and its contents from Reinforcement Exercise 3.

2. Double-click the **New Folder** icon, right-click the **Copy of New Folder** folder, drag it over to your Recycle Bin, drop it there, and then click on **Move Here**. Notice that the Recycle Bin indicates that it has contents.

3. Double-click the **Recycle Bin** to open it and view its contents.

4. Right-click the Copy of New Folder folder that you just discarded, and click on **Restore**.

5. Confirm that the Copy of New Folder folder did return to its previous location, inside the New Folder window. Close the Recycle Bin window.

6. Close the New Folder window, right-click on its icon on the desktop, click on **Delete**, and then click the **Yes** button to confirm the folder deletion.

7. Right-click the **Recycle Bin** icon, click on **Empty Recycle Bin**, and then click the **Yes** button to confirm the file deletion.

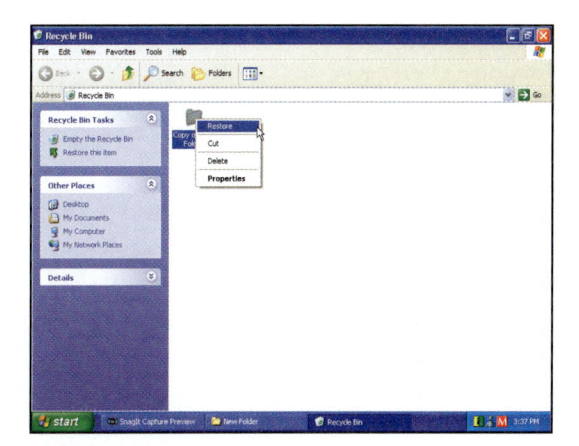

Reinforcement　WIN　**67**

CHALLENGE

Challenge exercises are designed to test your ability to apply your skills to new situations with less-detailed instructions. These exercises also challenge you to expand your repertoire of skills by using commands that are similar to those you already learned. The desired outcome is clearly defined, but you have more freedom to choose the steps needed to achieve the required result.

C1—Exploring the Windows Folder

In this lesson, you learned many of the navigation techniques used to locate objects on your computer. You should have noticed already that there are always multiple ways of accomplishing tasks in Windows XP. In this exercise, you will see how to view the contents of numerous objects by expanding and collapsing the hierarchical structure of your computer's contents using the Windows Explorer technique. Before starting this lesson, check with your instructor to make sure the Windows folder is viewable. If it is not, proceed to the next challenge exercise.

Goal: To explore the Windows folder.

1. Log on to your computer and click the **Start** button.

2. Point to the **All Programs** green arrow, then slide up the pull-out menu and point to **Accessories**.

3. In the pull-out menu to the right of Accessories, slide down to and click on **Windows Explorer** to open the My Documents window and reveal its contents in both the left and right panes.

4. Click the **My Music** folder in the left pane to highlight the folder and reveal its contents (if any) in the right pane.

5. Click back on the **My Documents** folder in the left pane to reveal its contents in the right pane. Click the minus (–) sign to the left of the now highlighted My Documents folder in the left pane to collapse the My Documents folder.

6. Click the plus (+) sign to the left of the **My Computer** folder in the left pane. Notice that the contents are not revealed in the right pane.

7. Click the minus (–) sign to the left of the **My Computer** folder in the left pane to collapse its contents. Notice once again that the contents are not revealed in the right pane.

8. Click the **My Computer** folder name in the left pane and notice that it both expands the folder's contents in the left pane and displays those contents in the right pane.

9. Expand the **Local Disk (C:)** folder by clicking its plus (+) sign in the left pane. Look for the **Windows** subfolder below the Local Disk folder (if necessary, use the scroll bar at the right side of the left pane to scroll down to the Windows folder) and click on that folder's name in the left pane. A *subfolder* is a folder embedded within another folder.

10. Continue expanding the folder hierarchy below the **Windows** folder (or the WINNT folder—depending on how your copy of Windows XP was installed on your computer) until there are no additional subfolders. Then, collapse the folders and click the **Close** button to close the window.

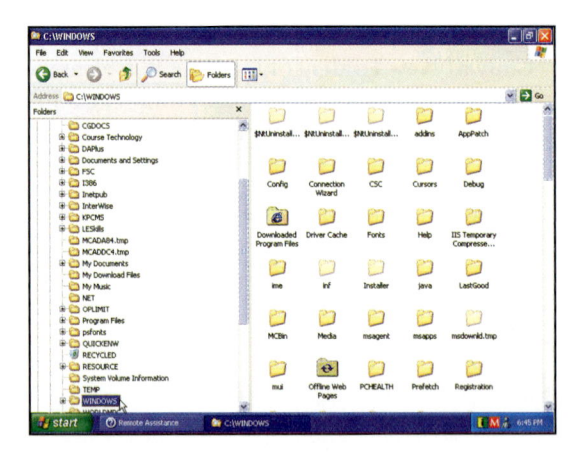

C2—Using Windows Explorer to View Microsoft's Web Site

Throughout this lesson, you learned the techniques for navigating to objects on your own computer. In this Challenge exercise you will see that you can use those same techniques to navigate to locations outside of not only your computer but also your building. You will navigate through your computer to a Web site located on the Internet.

Goal: To learn how to navigate to a Web site within My Computer.

1. Log on to your computer, and establish an Internet connection.

2. Click the **Start** button, right-click on **My Computer,** and then click on **Open** in the shortcut menu.

3. Right-click on **Local Disk (C:)** and select **Explore** in the shortcut menu.

4. In the address bar, enter the address for the Microsoft Web site (**http://www.microsoft.com**). Navigate the site's hyperlinks as desired and then click the green **Back arrow** one or more times to return to your initial starting point.

5. Click the **Close** button on the Welcome to the Microsoft Corporate Web Site window and the My Computer window to close them and put you back on the desktop.

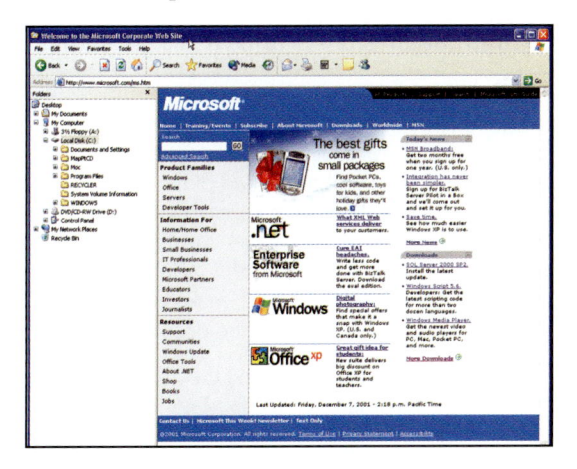

C3—Pinning an Application to the Start Menu

Much of what you learned about Windows XP so far has involved showing how easy it is to customize your environment. This Challenge exercise is no exception to that learning process. In this exercise you will learn the additional skill of being able to alter what is shown on the left side of the most frequently used menu in the Windows XP operating system—the Start menu. You will learn how to pin additional application icons to the top-left section of your Start menu.

Goal: To pin an application to the Start menu.

1. Log on to your local computer, and click the **Start** button.

2. Slide up the Start menu and right-click on one of your recently opened applications listed on the left side of your Start menu. A shortcut menu displays.

3. Click on **Pin to Start menu** in the shortcut menu. Your newly moved selection should be listed immediately in its new location, in the top section of the Start menu.

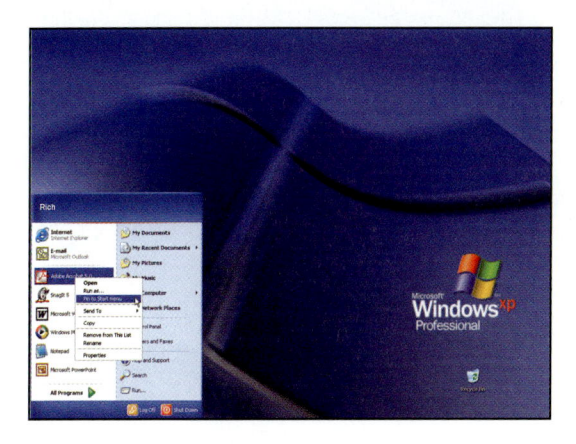

C4—Touring Windows XP

In this lesson, you learned how to work with the Help and Support Center. Microsoft has added quite a few more features to this section of its operating system. An important segment of these new features includes videos about the operating system itself. In this Challenge exercise, you learn to navigate to and view the video lesson that will give you a tour of Windows XP.

Goal: To use the Help and Support Center to tour Windows XP.

1. Log on to your computer. Then, click the **Start** button, and slide up to and click the **Help and Support** button (the blue question mark button) to activate the Help and Support Center.

2. Under the **Pick a Help topic** section, click on **What's new in Windows XP**.

3. In the left pane, click on **Taking a tour or tutorial**. In the right pane, click on **Take the Windows XP tour**.

4. In the Windows XP Tour dialog box, leave the default setting to play the animated tour and click on **Next**.

5. Allow the Introduction to play, and then click the **Windows XP Basics** button to start the tour.

6. At the end of the tour, the introduction will start again. Click the red X in the lower right corner of the window to exit the tour at any time, and return to the Help and Support Center.

7. Close the Help and Support Center window to return to your desktop.

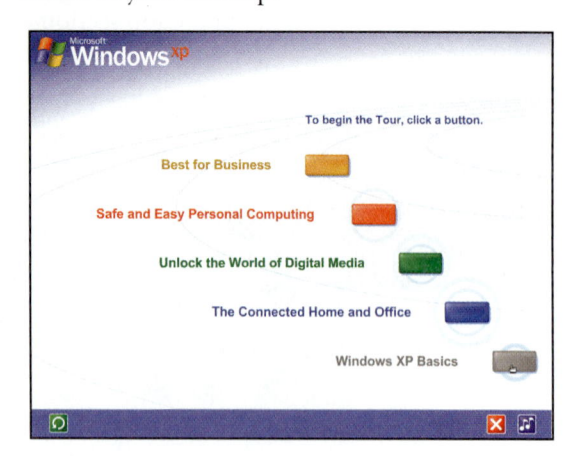

C5—Using Help to View a Listing of Shortcuts

In this lesson, you learned how to use several of the shortcuts available to you within Windows XP, such as the ones that provide quick access to objects from different locations on your computer, or those that are available through shortcut menus. There are many more that have not yet been discussed. Windows XP itself gives you more information about these shortcuts. In this Challenge exercise, you use the Help and Support Center to search for additional shortcuts.

Goal: To use the Help and Support Center to view a listing of shortcuts.

1. Log on to your computer. Then, click the **Start** button, and slide up to and click the **Help and Support** button (the blue question mark button) to activate the Help and Support Center.

2. In the **Search** text box, type **Windows keyboard shortcuts overview,** and click the green arrow (the Start searching button). This submits your request for the Help and Support Center to search its Help database and return all instances of the requested phrase. Note that it returns only one topic in the left Search Results pane.

3. Click on your phrase (now listed in blue) in the Search Results pane to retrieve the information regarding your query.

4. Starting with the **Windows Explorer keyboard shortcuts** listing and going upward, click the plus (+) sign to expand each of the five selections in the right pane.

5. Close the Help and Support Center window to return to your desktop.

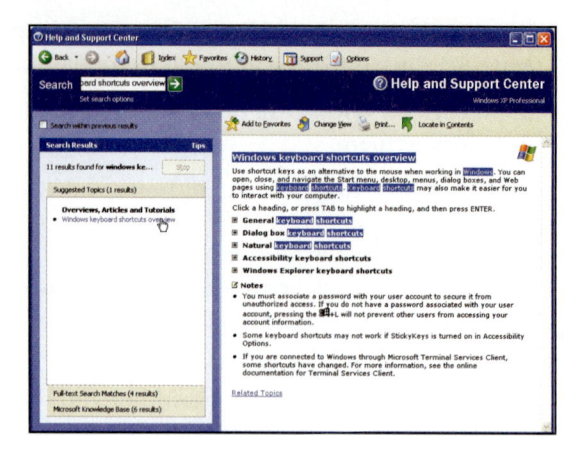

C6—Working with an Existing Application File

In this lesson, you learned how to use one of the application programs included in Windows XP. You opened the WordPad application, created a text document, saved it for later use, and even printed it for viewing. An important part of thoroughly using the Windows XP storage feature is the ability to retrieve your own document, make changes to it, save it with the changes, and print it with your changes incorporated. In this Challenge exercise, you open the previously saved document, make a change, save it with the change, print it, and then delete the document.

Goal: To open, alter, print, re-save, and then delete an already existing WordPad document (created in Task 8).

1. Log on to your computer. Then, click the **Start** button, and slide up to and click on **My Documents**.

2. Locate your document in the My Documents folder. (If it is not there, another user may have deleted it. Recreate the document by following the steps in Task 8.) Right-click the document's icon, and choose **Open With**, **WordPad** from the shortcut menu. Maximize the WordPad window, if necessary.

3. Click after the last line of text in the document, and press the ⏎Enter key twice. Then, choose **Help**, **About WordPad** in the menu bar.

4. Note that the information provided in the About WordPad dialog box includes a hyperlink to the **End-User License Agreement** (EULA). Click the hyperlink, skim through the EULA information displayed in WordPad, and then click the EULA's **Close** button.

5. Press Alt + Print Scrn to put a copy of the About WordPad dialog box on your *Clipboard* (a workspace you can use to store objects temporarily), and click the **OK** button.

6. Ensure that the cursor is blinking in the last line of your text document and type **I read the WordPad EULA—and survived!**

7. Press ⏎Enter twice, and press Ctrl+V to insert the About WordPad screen. Press Ctrl+S to save your changes, then print a copy of the document to submit to your instructor.

8. Click the **Close** button to exit the WordPad application. In the My Documents window, right-click your document's icon, click **Delete** in the shortcut menu, and click **Yes** to confirm the deletion. Close the My Documents window.

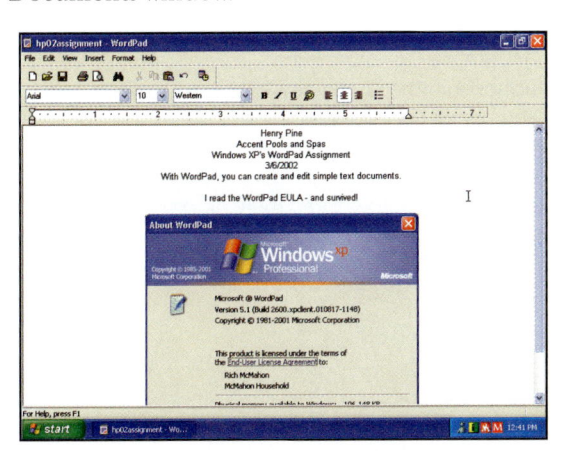

ON YOUR OWN

Expand on your knowledge about your keyboard. Start with the Help feature on your own computer and find more keyboard shortcuts (in addition to those listed in this lesson) to ease your workload. Print a copy of the shortcuts discussed in the Help feature and include them in the report discussed below. Additionally, Microsoft maintains an excellent resource site on the Web that you can visit to learn more about easier ways of working with keyboards (including additional shortcuts). The site's address is:

http://www.microsoft.com/enable/products/keyboard/keyboardsearch.asp

Once on that site, start with the Search for Tips and Tricks topic and gather information relating to shortcuts and ways to speed up working on your computer. Compile a complete list of keyboard actions that may help someone accomplish repetitive tasks they may have to perform at home, school, or work. Use this list as an appendix to the report that follows.

Continue searching the Microsoft site for links to additional information about keyboards. Look for information on new styles and features, while locating current articles (or white papers). Compile this information into a minimum three-page report on keyboard advances. That report should include information on new theories of ensuring accessibility for those with special needs. Save the report and print a copy for your instructor.

Glossary

Account types   Two different kinds of local user accounts in Windows XP that can be set up for you by the network administrator—the Computer Administrator account and Limited account.

Address bar   The drop-down list near the top of an object's window that can be used to access or search for resources either locally or on a network (including the Internet).

Administrative rights   Privileges that, when assigned to a user, afford him powers to maintain computers or networks that include installing all applications and hardware items, creating and controlling all user accounts, and making changes to the system's hardware or software architecture.

Case sensitive   A feature whereby passwords are verified by comparing the entry against the exact combination of uppercase and lowercase letters that were used when the password was created.

Click   The act of pressing and releasing the left mouse button. This action is often used to select an object or to place a cursor in the intended location.

Clipboard   A workspace you can use to temporarily store objects that you later paste or print to a new location.

Close button   The small red X button at the far right side of the title bar that closes the window or dialog box when you click it.

Collapsing   The act of clicking on the minus (–) sign when in the Windows Explorer mode, to remove the display of the contents of a folder in the window's left panel.

Computer administrator account   The more powerful of the two local user account types in Windows XP. This account type provides the user with administrative rights to the computer.

Control menu   A small drop-down menu (with access to minimize, maximize/restore, and close functions) that appears at the left end of a title bar when you press [Alt] + [Spacebar].

Control Panel   A feature that enables you to change many of your computer's settings using the Windows XP management tools stored there.

Cursor   In a graphical user environment, the cursor is usually a small arrow. The terms cursor and mouse pointer are often used interchangeably. When working with text, a cursor sometimes appears between the letters as an insertion point (an I-beam symbol).

Default   The initial settings which are automatically invoked when the operating system is installed. You can change many default settings to suit your own needs.

Desktop   A computer's version of the top of one's desk, where you can access and run the applications on your system via program icons, buttons on the taskbar, or the Start menu.

Double-click   The act of quickly pressing and releasing the left mouse button twice in succession. This action is usually used to execute an action, such as opening an application or highlighting a word in a document.

Drag and drop   The act of pointing to an item, clicking and holding the left mouse button down, moving the item, then releasing the mouse button.

Expanding   The act of clicking on a plus (+) sign when in the Windows Explorer mode, to display the contents of a folder in the window's left panel.

Floppy disk   A convenient and portable method for storing and retrieving computer data.

Floppy disk drive   The mechanism used to read or write information to or from a floppy disk.

Formatting   The action taken upon a computer storage medium, such as a floppy disk, that prepares the disk so that you can use it to store data for future use.

Gigabyte   The next larger unit of measurement above megabytes (MB). One gigabyte (GB) equals 1024 MB.

GUI (Graphical User Interface)   A user interface such as Windows XP that uses pictures in addition to text in order to be more user-friendly.

Hard disk drive   An internal component of your computer used for storage of applications and files that you save.

Hibernation   A method of resting your computer such that all the settings and the status of your applications and open documents are saved from memory to storage on your workstation's hard disk drive.

Hint   A clue that Windows XP provides to help you remember your password.

Home page   The Web page that initially displays when you start your browser.

Hotkeys   The hyperlinked letters in a drop-down menu that you can use to invoke the desired menu option using the keyboard.

Hyperlink   An item which, when clicked on, sends your browser to another corresponding Web page. On your own computer, these items can also be used to proceed immediately from one file to another that you have configured as a hyperlink.

Icon   A miniature graphical item, typically stored as a bitmap image, that represents an object such as a file, folder, or application in a graphical user interface environment. When you click or double-click the icon, you activate the object.

Insertion point   A blinking pointer (sometimes called a cursor) that appears at the location where you begin typing letters into your document.

Internet connection   A transmission path such as a phone line or network connection between your computer and the Internet.

Internet Explorer   The Internet browser program by Microsoft that comes with Windows XP.

Limited account   The more restrictive of the two local user account types in Windows XP. This account type has few administrative powers, but enables the user to make changes relating to their own account.

Log off   The act of ending a work session on a particular computer or terminating your network connection.

Log on   The act of fulfilling a computer system's security requirements to gain access to the computer or network. In Windows XP, a principal method of logging on involves clicking on the icon of a user's account and supplying a password (if one is used) to enable you to gain access to the computer.

Maximize/Restore button   The dual-purpose button immediately to the left of the Close button in the title bar that changes depending on whether or not the object is maximized. If the object doesn't fill the entire desktop, you can click the Maximize button to make the object fill the desktop. Once the object does fill the desktop, that same button becomes the Restore button and clicking it again puts the object back to the same size it was before you maximized it.

Menu bar   The horizontal bar that is typically displayed below the title bar and provides access to menu names such as File, Edit, View, Favorites, Tools, and Help.

Minimize button   The leftmost of the three buttons at the right end of the title bar. Clicking on that button reduces the object to becoming just a button on the taskbar.

Mouse pointer   A graphical symbol that allows a user to point to objects on the desktop by moving the mouse. It is usually in the shape of an arrow, but may change shapes as it points to objects in various applications.

My Computer   An application used to navigate and manage the files and folders stored on a Windows XP computer.

My Documents   A default folder used for storing files, folders, or other objects.

Network   A group of interconnected computers working together.

Notepad   A simple word-processing application included with Windows XP that displays a blank text area for text entry or retrieval.

Operating system   The software that controls the interface to peripheral hardware, allocates storage, schedules tasks, and gives a default interface to the user when no applications are running. Windows XP is an operating system.

Panes   The panels or frames in a window. In My Computer, the left pane displays information items grouped together, and the right pane displays the objects within the item selected in the left pane.

Peripheral device   An add-on computer component, such as a printer or scanner.

Point   The act of sliding the mouse so that the mouse pointer moves to the intended object.

Pop-up description   A display that appears after pausing your mouse pointer over an item.

Recycle Bin   An icon on the desktop that simulates the functions of a trash can. It enables the user to discard objects that aren't needed and has the ability of allowing discarded object retrieval if thus configured.

Remote Assistance   A new feature available with Windows XP that allows an operator on one computer to take control of another computer (as long as both are operating under Windows XP) to help with a problem.

Right-click   The act of pressing and releasing the right mouse button. This action is usually used to activate a context-sensitive menu, called a shortcut menu, that applies to the intended object.

Screen saver A feature that helps prevent images from being burned in to the monitor's screen. It runs in the background without degrading or appreciably slowing down the computer's operating capability.

Shortcut menu A context-sensitive menu activated by pointing to text, a screen element, or an object, and right-clicking the mouse button.

Sleeping A power-saving function of a monitor. The monitor can be left on, but this feature limits its power consumption. It is usually shown by a red or amber power-saver indicator light.

Start button A method used to gain access to applications and functions on your computer. The Start button is the green button located at the left end of the taskbar.

Start menu The menu that allows the user access to the computer's applications after the Start button is clicked.

Subfolder A folder embedded within another folder.

Switch User option An option that enables you to leave your current applications or opened objects in their current state while you allow another user (who is also authorized on that workstation) to log on to the workstation.

System administrator The person usually in charge of installing and maintaining your computer and possibly the network if your computer is on one.

Taskbar The horizontal bar at the bottom of the screen containing items such as the Start button and taskbar buttons indicating which applications are open.

Title bar The horizontal bar at the top of a window or dialog box that contains the control menu icon, the name of the document and/or application, and the Minimize, Maximize/Restore, and Close buttons.

Toolbar A common component of a graphical user interface, consisting of a visible row of button icons, which allows the user to perform common tasks more quickly than using the menu bar.

Toolbar buttons A function of the toolbar that provides one-click access to many of the most common actions you are able to perform when using the pull-down menus on the menu bar.

Triple-click The act of quickly pressing and releasing the left mouse button three times in succession. This action is usually used inside text to highlight a block of text, such as a paragraph.

Views button A toolbar button that, when available, lets you change the way you see the items displayed inside the object you are working with.

Window The graphical view of an active object such as an open folder, dialog box, or application.

Windows Explorer A hierarchy-based application for navigating and managing the filing system on your Windows XP computer.

Windows logo key A special key recently added to the keyboards of most computers. Pressing ⊞ invokes shortcuts usually intended for Microsoft functionality. In particular, this key provides a quick way to activate the Start menu.

Windows Welcome screen Usually the first screen encountered when logging on to a Windows XP computer. It typically shows the names of that computer's users.

WordPad A higher-level word-processing application than Notepad, that is also included with Windows XP.

Index

A

Accessories menu, accessing, 9
accounts, user
   adding, 30
   creating new, 32
address bar, 10
   Web site addresses on, 34
addresses, for Web sites, entering, 34
administrative rights, 21
administrative user, logging in as, 44
Advanced tab (Customize Start Menu dialog box), 52
All files and folders option (Search Results window), 55
All Programs option (Start menu), 9
Alt+spacebar keystrokes, 40
applications, on Start menu
   adding to menu, 69
   opening, 60
   viewing, 9
Apply button (dialog boxes), 13
arrow button, 5

B

Back button, navigating windows using, 45
backgrounds, customizing on desktops, 19
backspace key, 60
blue question mark button, 5
buttons, on toolbars, 10

C

Cancel button, 13
   in Turn Off Computer dialog box, 26
case sensitivity of passwords, 5
centering text, in WordPad, 61
Change Picture button (User Accounts window), 20
Clear List button (Customize Start Menu dialog box), 52
click action (mouse), 6
Clipboard, 70
Close button (title bar), 39
Close Group option (My Computer window), 45

closing
   folders/files, 42
   WordPad program, 63
collapsing folders, 49
computer
   hibernation, 25
   turning off, 22
   waking up, 4
computer administrator account, 20
configuration settings, defaults, 47
Confirm File Delete dialog box (Recycle Bin), 18
Control menu, 40
Control Panel (User Accounts window)
   adding new user account, 30
   changing switch user options, 30-31
Control Panel
   accessing, 10
   Display pointer trails option, 7
   Mouse Properties dialog box
      mouse icon, 11
      Speed adjustment slider, 11
   Printers and Other Hardware folder, 11
   User Accounts window, 19
      creating new user accounts, 32
Ctrl+P keystrokes, 63
Customize Start menu dialog box (Start menu), 52
   Advanced tab, 52
   Clear List button, 52
   selecting/clearing start options, 53
customizing desktops
   backgrounds, 19
   Recycle Bin settings, 12-14

D

Date/Time button (toolbar), 60
defaults
   folder windows, 47
   My Documents folder, 39
   Recycle Bin, 12-13
   for searches, 55-56
   start up screen saver, 3, 30
deleting
   confirm message, 13, 18
   folders, 17, 34, 67
desktop
   creating new folders, 14-16
   customizing backgrounds, 19

   customizing Recycle Bin settings, 12-14
   deleting folders from, 17
   icons on, moving, 8
   navigating, mouse for, 6
Details section (My Computer), 54
devices, peripheral, 1
dialog boxes, Apply and Cancel buttons, 13
directory trees, plus and minus signs in, 49
Display as menu option (Customize Start Menu dialog box), 52
Display pointer trails option (Control Panel), 7
Display Properties dialog box, Screen Saver tab, 30
documents
   locating using search feature, 55-56
   in WordPad
      creating documents using, 33
      editing, 70-71
      previewing, 62
      printing, 63
      saving, 63
Documents and Settings folder, opening, 44, 48
double-click action (mouse), 6
double-headed arrow, 41-42
drag and drop action (mouse), 6
   moving folders, 66
   relocating text using, 61

E

editing WordPad documents, 60, 70-71
emptying Recycle Bin, 18, 67
End-User License Agreement (EULA), for WordPad, 70
Enter key, 11
expanding folders, 49

F

File menu
   Print button, 63
   Save As button, 63
   Save button, 63
files
   creating using Notepad, 33
   storing in My Documents folder, 39

floppy disk drives, 57
floppy disks
   formatting, 57-58
      format options, 59
      format process, 59
      Quick Format options, 58
   high density disks, 57
   uses for, 56
Folder Options dialog box (Tools menu), 16-17
   Open each folder in its own window option, 46
folders
   adding new folders, 14-15
   closing, options for, 42
   creating, 33
   customizing, 15-16
   deleting, 17, 67
   for each user name, viewing, 45
   expanding/collapsing views of, 49
   locating using search feature, 55-56
   moving, 66
   opening
      default configuration, 47
      keyboard shortcuts for, 11
   renaming, 15, 66
   restoring from Recycle Bin, 67
   shortcuts to, identifying, 49
   storing in My Documents, 39
   Windows folder, accessing/exploring, 68
Format a floppy disk command, 58
Format Complete dialog box, 59
formatting
   floppy disks, 57-58
      format options, 59
      format process, 59
      Quick Format options, 58
   text
      in Notepad, 33
      in WordPad, 61
Forward button, navigating through windows using, 45
frames in windows, 10

G

graphical user interface (GUI), 6

H

hard disk drive, opening from My Computer, 44

hard drive, viewing information about, 54
Help and Support Center, opening, 58
help system
   accessing, keyboard shortcuts for, 58
   blue question mark button, 5
   list of keyboard shortcuts, 70
   pop-up description boxes, 23, 25
   touring Windows XP, 69-70
   WordPad Help, 62
Hibernate button (Turn Off Computer dialog box), 25, 31
hibernation, when to use, 25
high density (HD) floppy disks, 57
hints, attaching to passwords, 5
home page, 34
horizontal tiling, 62
hyperlinks, 34

I

I-bar (vertical bar) pointer, 61
icons
   defined, 8
   hard disk drive, 54
   Maximize versus Restore button, 40
   My Documents, 39
   on desktops, moving using mouse, 8
   selecting using Tab key, 11
   shortcuts to folders, 49
   toolbar buttons, 10
Icons view (View menu), 42
insertion point, 33
interface, user, 6
Internet
   connecting to, 34
   entering Web site addresses, 34
   home page, 34
Internet Explorer, opening, 34

K

keyboard shortcuts
   for changing users, 23
   help system tools, 58
   Log Off button, 22
   menu items, activating, 15
   Minimize/Maximize/Close options, 40
   obtaining list of, 70
   for opening local hard drives, 47
   for opening/closing folders, 11
   for opening/closing Start menu, 8
   printing, 63

L

left pane (My Computer window), 43
locking computers, preventing access, 23
Log Off button (Start menu), 22-23
Log On to Windows dialog box, 4
logging off, 21
logging on, 3
   network systems, 4
   passwords, 4-5
   selecting user name, 4
   Windows Welcome screen, 4

M

Maximize/Restore button (title bar), 39-40
menu bar, 10
menus, activating items in, shortcuts for, 15
Minimize button (title bar), 39-40
minus (–) sign, in collapsed folders, 49
monitors
   power options, 32
   sleep mode, 3
mouse
   click action, 6
   double-click action, 6
   drag and drop action, 6
      moving folders, 66
      relocating text, 61
   moving icons using, 8
   navigating desktop using, 6
   opening Start menu using, 8
   right click action, 6
   settings for, changing, 9
   speed settings, 11
   triple-click action, 6
   waking computer using, 4
mouse pointer, 4
   displaying trails, 7
   double-headed arrow, 41
   I-bar (vertical bar), 61
   insertion points, 33
   locating, 7
   passing over objects with, 49
   using with accuracy, 7
Mouse Properties dialog box (Control Panel), 11
moving
   desktop icons, 8
   folders, 66
   text in WordPad, 61
multiple users, start up for, 4

My Computer folder
accessing My Documents folder, 45, 47
accessing objects
Documents and Settings folder, 44
hard disk drive, 44
accessing Web sites, 68-69
Close Group option, 45
formatting floppy disks, 57-59
organization of, 43
viewing contents, 68
viewing system information, 54

My Documents folder, 39
creating new folder in, 33
Explore view, accessing, 48
opening from My Computer window, 45
opening multiple times, 48
resizing window for, 41-42
viewing contents, 68

My Music folder, viewing contents, 68

N

names, of folders, viewing, 10
naming new folders, 15
navigating Web sites, 34
navigating Windows
moving between views, 46
My Computer, 37
Windows Explorer for, 37, 46
networks, startup screens, 4
Notepad program, 33
closing, 34

O

Open each folder in its own window option (Tools menu, Folder Options), 46
operating system, defined, 1
output from searches (Search Results window), 56

P

panes, 10
passwords
adding to User accounts, 20
attaching hints to, 5
case sensitivity, 5
supplying at log in, 4-5

performance, and number of active users, 23
peripheral devices, 1
Pin to Start menu option (Start menu), 69
plus (+) sign, in expanded directory view, 49
pointers
double-headed arrow, 41-42
I-bar (vertical bar) pointer, 61
pop-up description boxes, 10, 23
pop-up information boxes, 4
pop-up menus, 9
Power Options Properties dialog box (Power button), 32-33
power saver feature, 3
Power schemes, 32
previewing WordPad documents, 62
Print button (File menu), 63
Print Preview button (toolbar), 62
Printers and Other Hardware folder (Control Panel), 11
printing WordPad documents, 63
Properties option (Start menu), 50-51

Q

Quick Format option, 58

R

Recycle Bin
changing settings for, 12-14
emptying, 18, 67
moving folders to, 67
restoring folders/files in, 67
sending deleted items to, 17
Recycle Bin Properties dialog box, changing default settings, 12-13
Remote Assistance feature, 39
Rename option (shortcut menu), 66
renaming
floppy disk labels, 57
folders, 15, 66
resizing windows, 40
double-headed arrows for, 41-42
Restart button (Turn Off Computer dialog box), 25–26
Restore Down option (Maximize/Restore button), 40
restoring
deleted folders, 67
windows, 40

right click action (mouse), 6
accessing shortcut menus, 12
right pane (My Computer window), 43

S

Save As button (File menu), 63
Save button (File menu), 63
saving WordPad documents, 63
screen saver, default at startup, changing, 3, 30
Screen Saver tab (Display Properties dialog box), 30
screen savers, 3
scroll bar (Start menu), 52
Search Results window (Start menu), 55
All files and folders option, 55
identifying search location, 55-56
output, 56
searching
folders, 55
Search Results window for
accessing window, 55
initiating search, 56
output, 56
selecting location for, 55
security tools, passwords, 4-5
setup, default, 3
changing screen saver, 30
shortcut menu
accessing using mouse, 6
adding new folders using, 14-15
desktop, monitor power settings, 32-33
Recycle Bin, Properties option, 12-13
Rename option, 66
Start menu
Pin to Start menu option, 69
Properties option, 50-51
shortcuts, icons for, 49
Shut Down Computer button, 22
shut down procedures, 25
sleep mode, 3
Speed adjustment slider (Mouse Properties dialog box), 11
Start button, 8
Start menu
accessing Control Panel from, 10
Accessories submenu, 60
adding applications to, 69
All Programs option, 9
customizing
accessing Properties option, 50-51
Customize Start menu dialog box, 52-53

Log Off button, 22
opening
keyboard shortcuts, 8
mouse for, 8
Search Results window, 55
start up. *See also* **logging on**
default settings
screen saver, 3, 30
viewing list of users, 4
subfolders, 68
Switch User button, 23
uses for, 24
switching users
options for, 30-31
during shut down process, 23
system administrator, 3
system information, viewing, 54

T

Tab key, selecting icons using, 11
taskbar, defined, 8
text
in Notepad, 33
in WordPad
editing, 60
entering, 60
formatting, 61
previewing document, 62
thumbnail views, activating, 42
tiling windows, 62
title bar, 10
icons on, 40
Maximize/Restore button, 40
Minimize button, 40
toolbar
buttons on, 10
Date/Time button, 60
Print Preview button, 62
Views button, 42
Tools menu, Folder Options, 46
touring Windows XP, 69-70
triple-click action (mouse), 6
Turn Off Computer button (Log Off button), 22, 24
Cancel button, 26
Hibernate button, 25, 31

Restart button, 26
Turn Off button, 25
turning on computer, 3
tutorials, Windows XP tour, 69-70

U

user accounts
adding new accounts, 30, 32
types of, 20
User accounts window (Control Panel), 19-20
adding new accounts, 30
Change Picture button, 20
Change the way users log on or off options, 30-31
user interface, 6
user names
selecting at start up, 4
viewing at startup, 4
viewing folders associated with, 45
users, switching
changing during shut down process, 23
changing options for, 30-31

V

vertical bar pointer (I-bar), 61
viewing full screen in WordPad, 61
views, navigating between, 46
Views button (toolbar)
Icons view, 42
Thumbnails option, 42
Volume label (floppy disks), 57

W

"waking up" the computer, 4
Web sites
accessing from My Computer, 68-69
entering addresses for, 34
navigating, 34

windows
closing
closing all open windows, 48
options for, 42
expanded views, 54
frames, 10
names of, viewing, 10
navigating, 37
buttons for, 45
resizing, 41-42
restoring/resizing, 40
tiling, 62
Windows Explorer, 37, 46
accessing from My Documents folder, 48
opening, 46
Windows folder, accessing/exploring, 68
Windows logo key, 8
Windows Welcome screen, 4
Windows XP, virtual tour of, 69-70
WinKey, changing users using, 23
word wrapping, applying to text, 33
WordPad program, 37
accessing/editing existing documents, 70-71
closing, 63
help tools for, 62
opening, 60
saving documents, 63
using
adding text, 60
editing text, 60
formatting text, 61
previewing document, 62
printing document, 63

Z

Zoom In button (Print Preview window), 62